A BETTE
TEACH KIDS ABOUT SEX

Laura M. Padilla-Walker, Ph.D.
Dean M. Busby, Ph.D.
Chelom E. Leavitt, Ph.D.
Jason S. Carroll, Ph.D.

DESERET BOOK
Salt Lake City, Utah

Illustrations provided by the authors.

Visit us at DeseretBook.com

Library of Congress Cataloging-in-Publication Data

Names: Padilla-Walker, Laura M., author. | Busby, Dean M., author. | Leavitt, Chelom Eastwood, 1967– author. | Carroll, Jason S., author.

Title: A better way to teach kids about sex / Laura M. Padilla-Walker, Ph.D., Dean M. Busby, Ph.D., Chelom E. Leavitt, Ph.D., Jason S. Carroll, Ph.D.

Description: Salt Lake City, Utah : Deseret Book, [2018] | Includes bibliographical references.

Identifiers: LCCN 2018008902 | ISBN 9781629723730 (paperbound)

Subjects: LCSH: Sex instruction—Religious aspects—The Church of Jesus Christ of Latter-day Saints. | Parenting—Religious aspects—The Church of Jesus Christ of Latter-day Saints.

Classification: LCC BX8643.S49 P33 2018 | DDC 241/.664071—dc23

LC record available at https://lccn.loc.gov/2018008902

Printed in the United States of America

PubLitho, Draper, UT

10 9 8 7 6 5 4 3 2 1

Contents

Introduction

Welcome to *A Better Way to Teach Kids about Sex*! It's possible that you're picking up this book because your child is struggling with sexuality and you are searching for answers. Or perhaps your ten-year-old just came home and told you he's been holding hands with his "girlfriend" at school and you can no longer deny that your child is a sexual being, so you want to better understand how to have "the talk." Or maybe you just want to start when your children are very young in hopes of having the best chance at raising sexually healthy children.

Whatever your reason is for searching, we hope this book will provide you answers and a way to talk about sexuality with your children and teenagers that is specifically tailored for the current reality in which they are growing up (which is much different than what our reality was when we were young). We hope to dispel myths and cultural practices that have become almost commonplace in our culture but that often do more harm than good. And most of all, it is our desire to help you see that the astonishing transformation children experience as they become sexual beings is not something that you should dread or fear, but rather a fantastic miracle to celebrate and enjoy. Wherever you are and whatever is worrying you about your child, our goal with this book is to help you feel more comfort and peace and to give you the tools you will need to help your child successfully navigate his or her sexual journey.

Can you think back to how your parents taught you about sex? Maybe they did a great job, maybe there were a few things lacking, perhaps you and your siblings joke about it now, or it might have even been a disaster. In this book, we approach sexuality in a way that might be different from the ways it has been dealt with in the past, and our belief and hope is that this is a better way that will help us to raise children who do not just abstain from sex but who are also sexually healthy. This is important because healthy sexuality goes beyond merely abstaining from sexual activity—though that is an important place to start. Countless youth have abstained from premarital sex only to find themselves in the midst of a marriage that is filled with sexual problems and hang-ups that threaten the very fabric of their families. The goal of this book is to raise children who are both sexually pure *and* sexually prepared.

As parents, most of us have embraced the importance of sexual purity, but we might be less comfortable helping our children prepare themselves to be sexually healthy in mind, body, and spirit. However, most would agree that we want each of our children to develop into adults with healthy sexual attitudes and behaviors that are expressed freely within a committed marriage. This is why we use terms such as "healthy sexuality" or "sexual wholeness" as something for which we all should strive. When the time comes, we want our children to enjoy, appreciate, and flourish in the sexual area and help their future children do likewise.

So what things might still be holding us back? We might have a great desire to encourage healthy sexuality but feel all too aware that our own ideas about sexuality are not healthy and worry that our fears and anxieties will negatively influence how we teach our children. First, it is important for parents to understand that it is not a requirement to be perfectly sexually healthy in order to teach about healthy sexuality. But in many cases, improving one's own sexual health will help ease the discomfort of teaching a child. So we will offer some general principles and suggest additional resources for parents who feel they would like to challenge some of their own beliefs about sexuality at the same time that they're striving to help a child understand his or her emerging sexuality.

Some parents may also feel that they're starting this process too early or too late. For those parents of young children, please know that it is never too early to start setting healthy patterns of talking to your child about sexuality in developmentally appropriate ways. In fact, the earlier, the better. That being said, it is also *never too late* to begin being more open with your children about sexuality. An important reminder for parents comes from Elder Bradley D. Foster, who said, "I know I can't turn back time, but this I now know—that it's never too early and it's never too late to lead, guide, and walk beside our children, because families are forever."[1] Every step in the right direction that is taken will help our children develop healthy sexuality, even if we aren't fully confident or we feel we have done things incorrectly in the past. There may be some unlearning that has to occur as we try to establish a new and better climate in our homes around the topic of sexuality—there is no use in feeling guilt about this. The best we can do is move forward and do a little better with the day we have before us.

To give you a more specific idea of what we'll tackle in this book, we will first provide a brief overview. Most of us have been exposed to far too many unhelpful sexual metaphors that we will dispel in this book. In their place, we will offer suggestions for more effective ways to communicate with young people about sexuality. We will then share our model for sexual wholeness, which will help guide our discussion about sexuality and inform the ways you approach your children about this topic. We offer both broad and specific suggestions for parents about how to approach conversations and questions about sexuality with children that will help parents feel more comfortable with and confident in this aspect of their role as a parent (especially as it relates to children who likely have different personalities and will thus need slightly different approaches). We will explain in some detail the physical changes that are taking place for your child, and we will offer suggestions about how you might navigate and celebrate puberty. We will discuss important topics related to sexuality, such as body image, modesty, masturbation, pornography, and sexual orientation, and share both scientific research and gospel truths to help give you the tools necessary to raise sexually healthy children. Finally, we will discuss chastity while dating and ways in which we can still help our children when they are approaching their wedding night. Throughout the book we seek to offer specific suggestions or tactics that you can try with your children until you find your own approaches and are completely comfortable discussing sexuality with your child. We are excited to be on this most important journey with those who share our care and concern, so let us begin!

SECTION 1

BUILDING A FOUNDATION

Chapter 1

Sexual Metaphors

Why all those youth conference analogies of chewed gum and unwrapped cupcakes did more harm than good.

Many people have built collections of various types. Some people like to collect stamps, others collect coins, and some collect spoons. However, our collection is different than most; ours is a collection of hundreds of personal stories from young adults in the Church telling us how they were taught about sexuality. For several years now, we have asked our students and others to share with us how and what they learned about this topic, and we have carefully collected their stories.

We have found that sharing the insights we have gained while accumulating these stories is helpful in teaching couples how to develop sexual wholeness in marriage. However, we believe that these stories may be even more relevant to providing insights into how we can raise sexually healthy children. This is because these very personal accounts offer a unique window into the sexual culture of many LDS homes and wards. We are particularly intrigued by how frequently we are told by young people that their parents and Church leaders used *object lessons* to teach them about sexuality. These lessons are highly symbolic and tend to compare sex to an object or a pattern of behavior. Much can be learned from understanding the metaphors and messages that are intentionally—and unintentionally—expressed in these types of lessons. Nearly all of the object lessons we have been told about can be grouped into two main categories: 1) fear-based metaphors, and 2) abstinence-based metaphors. So as we tell you about these personal accounts, reflect on your own experiences in learning about sexuality. Is your experience similar to any of those we describe? And as a parent, do any of these accounts reflect the ways that you are teaching about sexuality in your home?

Fear-Based Metaphors

The "fear-based metaphor" label is not meant to imply that the parents, youth leaders, or seminary teachers who have used these object lessons were trying to frighten their young learners. In fact, we are confident that the individuals who used these types of object lessons were well-intending people who were just trying to impress an important concept upon the minds of their children or class members. Nevertheless, and in spite of the good intentions of the teachers, we have been told over and over again that such lessons caused most of the listeners to have feelings of fear and anxiety and to receive other unintended negative messages about sexuality. This is unfortunate, because the Lord has taught that "if ye are prepared, ye shall not fear" (D&C 38:30). He did not say, "If ye are fearful, ye shall be prepared."

Fear-based metaphors typically compare sex to something being damaged or being made unclean. For example, a seminary teacher once showed a class a delicious, wrapped cupcake and asked if any of them would like to eat it. After many students enthusiastically said they wanted the treat, the teacher unwrapped the cupcake and had them pass it around. After each person had handled it, the seminary teacher asked, "Who would like to eat the cupcake *now*?" Of course, the point of the lesson was clear: the cupcake had become "unclean" and, therefore, undesirable. The instructor then compared the "handled cupcake" to the impurity of sexual involvement before marriage.

Another version of this type of object lesson uses chewing gum as the metaphor. In yet another, flowers were used: after all of the class members had touched the delicate petals, they soon wilted and turned brown. Again, the parallel was drawn that such inappropriate "touching" spoiled a beautiful thing, leaving it wilted and damaged. Another young woman told us about an object lesson that was used at a girls' camp. As the leaders and young women gathered around the fire (a genuine fireside!), a beautiful white wedding dress was brought out and held up as a symbol of being clean and pure on one's wedding day. During the lesson, however, as examples of immodest and unworthy behaviors were discussed, portions of the dress were then cut out and thrown into the campfire.

Perhaps the most dramatic fear-based object lesson we have been told about occurred in a Young Women lesson where the leader was comparing personal purity to a beautiful china plate. As she showed the girls the plate, she encouraged them to admire its beauty and fine craftsmanship. She extolled its uniqueness and noted that it was worth a very high price. Then, without warning, the leader turned and threw the plate against the wall, shattering it into pieces! The girls were then told that to be sexually impure before marriage was similar to throwing their "purity plate" against a wall—thus shattering something of great worth.

A Negative Portrayal of Sexual Intimacy

Certainly not all fear-based metaphors involve shattering plates, burning wedding dresses, or contaminating food. However, one of the primary consequences of fear-based object lessons and metaphors about sexuality is a negative portrayal of sexual intimacy, often unintentionally conveying to young minds that sex is a bad thing that harms us. While sexual sin clearly has negative effects on our lives, fear-based object lessons typically don't include a balanced discussion about the positive consequences associated with healthy sexuality. Even when a balanced view of sexuality is presented, many young people have told us that the negative feelings created from such object lessons are so overwhelming that they struggle to internalize any other messages from the lesson.

Latter-day Saint young people have also told us that when parents and leaders appeared uneasy or reluctant to teach them about sex, they began to feel apprehensive about the topic themselves. In fact, it is quite clear that many parents and leaders like to use object lessons because it allows them to talk about sex—without talking about sex. If young people internalize these fretful emotions, such negative conditioning may have long-term consequences in later marriages when couples try to "re-program" their attitudes about modesty, sexuality, and intimacy inside their relationship. They also have negative consequences for parenting as too many of us find ourselves feeling awkward and embarrassed about the topic, just as our parents were.

Fear-based metaphors also tend to discourage an open

dialogue between young people and their parents about sexuality. Often in this context, young people feel that if they ask questions or show any interest in the topic, they may be thought of as "bad" or "dirty." Thus, we shouldn't be surprised when young people gravitate to friends, the media, or other outside sources to learn about sexual issues—sources that are often not in harmony with gospel values. Their personal experiences learning about sexual matters then become mostly secretive, and they recall reading anatomy books, watching TV programs, or doing Internet searches under a cloak of secrecy, embarrassment, and shame. This, of course, is the opposite of what we should be striving for as parents. As Sister Cheryl A. Esplin explained, "Sometimes the most powerful way to teach our children to understand a doctrine is to teach in the context of what they are experiencing right at that moment. These moments are spontaneous and unplanned and happen in the normal flow of family life. . . . We need to be alert and recognize a teaching moment when our children come to us with a question or worry."[1]

Fear-based metaphors tend to teach about out-of-bounds behaviors (e.g., "sex before marriage is wrong," "masturbation is sinful," "don't use pornography," etc.), but they struggle to convey the doctrinal principles or reasons behind these restrictions. This often leaves young people unpersuaded as to why they should try to live a sexually pure life—particularly in a world that is becoming more adept at inviting them to be unchaste. Many young people have also commented to us that fear-based metaphors made them feel that there was no way they could repent of or repair any sexual missteps they may have already committed. The only message they heard was the ideal of flawless sexual perfection, rather than one of sincere sexual progression. To young minds, images of burned dresses and wilted flower petals appear irreparable and permanent. Thus, some are left to feel that they are the damaged goods that no one—including their Father in Heaven—will ever want. These messages are particularly harmful to young people who have experienced sexual abuse or trauma and may mistakenly believe that these metaphors are describing them. Our children need to be sincerely taught "that Jesus Christ is the Great Healer of our souls. . . . There is no sin or transgression, pain or sorrow, which is outside of the healing power of His Atonement."[2]

Abstinence-Based Metaphors

While parents and leaders sometimes teach young people about sexuality using fear-based metaphors, our experience is that the more common object lessons fit into a group we call "abstinence-based metaphors." These metaphors convey a "worth-waiting-for" message to young people, in which sex is portrayed as a positive aspect of life when experienced within the context of marriage. For some reason, many abstinence-based metaphors involve desirable food. For example, a counselor in the bishopric once brought freshly baked chocolate chip cookies to a combined youth lesson about chastity—on a fast Sunday. As the aroma of the cookies spread throughout the room, he asked the youth if they would like to eat one. After they eagerly indicated they would love to have one of the cookies, the counselor reminded the group that it was fast Sunday. After their groans had subsided, the counselor compared waiting to eat the cookies at the right time to waiting until marriage for sex.

Another young man told us about his deacons quorum

adviser, who gave each young man two chocolate candies and told them, “If you bring these chocolates back next week, I’ll give you ten chocolates.” So the following week the boys who brought both their candies back were rewarded with the promised ten chocolates. Then the adviser said, “Now, for those who bring all ten chocolates back next week, I’ll give you a whole bag of chocolates.” You can see where the adviser was going with this, right? At the end of the third week, the adviser used the example to teach the boys that delayed gratification brings bigger rewards and greater satisfactions compared to immediate gratification, and encouraged them to wait for the “bigger treat” that awaits them in marriage.

Now, you may be wondering what is so wrong with such abstinence-based metaphors. After all, is there a better symbol of goodness and happiness than warm chocolate chip cookies?! Despite their appealing images, the flaw with these object lessons is rooted in what they fail to teach rather than in what they do teach. They are only partially correct, because they are incomplete metaphors. Our interviews over the years have convinced us that such abstinence-based lessons may have a number of unintended negative side effects.

Chastity Is Viewed as Simply a Physical Issue

One of the primary pitfalls of abstinence-based lessons is that they unintentionally imply that chastity is simply a physical issue. The focus is on just sexual behaviors and the timing of such behaviors. While behaviors are an important part of the law of chastity, they are not the heart of the law. Chastity and virtue are at the heart of the law, thus making it more of a spiritual issue that should first be embraced in our hearts and our minds before it is expressed in our behaviors. Unfortunately, abstinence-based object lessons tend to assume that all expressions of sexuality are similar in intent and purpose. And there is typically no acknowledgment that both loving and lustful approaches to sexuality may occur even after marriage. They incorrectly assume that all sexual expressions after marriage are inherently loving in nature—simply because they take place after a wedding. What is also not taught is that attitudes and motives regarding why spouses seek sexual union with each other can change, and thus these become the true indicator of whether sexual behaviors are chaste or not. We may be chaste both before and after we are married; we may also be unchaste before or after marriage, and actions alone do not determine the difference. Simply put, the *whys* of sex in marriage matter more than the *whats* of sex. Chasity isn't just about *when* sex happens; it's about *why* it happens. We hope that in marriage, sex will be shared for the right reasons, but that requires a deeper and fuller understanding of healthy sexuality—one in which spouses are never compared to a cookie!

Perhaps the most troubling aspect of abstinence-based metaphors is that they convey the mistaken idea that the need for chastity ends at marriage. They teach young people that if they can "just hold out" until they are married, they will not have to worry about chastity any more. Perhaps such reasoning motivates some couples to shorten their engagements and get married before they "make a mistake." There is no such thing as a marriage finish line with respect to chastity and personal purity. Chastity is one of the ongoing foundational principles of healthy and lasting marriages. Couples should be taught to keep their thoughts and actions chaste even on their honeymoons and into their marriages. So when understood correctly, marriage is not the end but a continuation of our quest for chastity and personal purity.

Chastity Is Viewed as Simply an Individual Issue

Abstinence-based perspectives also tend to portray chastity as a character trait that one earns as a result of wise personal choices and worthiness. But a deeper appreciation of chastity is found in relationships between two people. Chastity is relational in nature because sex is designed to be an experience that involves another and can thus convey either other-centered love or self-centered lust. When sex is compared to one person eating something such as food or candy, it implies that true sexual fulfillment comes from receiving, not from giving. Thus, the sharing and other-centered aspects of sexuality are missing, and these are the key components that are vital in building a healthy and intimate marriage.

We need to help our children understand that the divine purpose of sexual intimacy is to unify spouses and strengthen the marital bond; we are not simply to be chaste for the sake of being chaste. Therefore, we need to define sexuality both in terms of emotional and physical forms of intimate expressions and in personal and relationship terms. Intimacy is connected to "shared vulnerability," in which people reveal themselves to each other and feel nurtured and cared for in their interactions. This type of revealing happens in relationships where partners can talk, share, and disclose to each other as well as be physically close with each other. So, when we talk about sexual intimacy and chastity, we should think about relationship behaviors broadly—not just the physical behaviors typically defined as personal rules or standards.

A New Metaphor

You may be thinking, *What, then, is an appropriate object lesson to use? What would be the best metaphor to properly teach about sexuality?* Our counter-culture answer to this question is that the best object lesson is no object lesson! Even if someone comes up with a clever object lesson that seems to get past the pitfalls of fear-based and abstinence-based metaphors, using *any* object lesson still conveys that as a parent or youth instructor you are uncomfortable with directly addressing the topic of sexuality. We are repeatedly told by young people that their great wish is to have their parents and leaders simply talk to them openly—and thoroughly—about sex. In short, there is no adequate metaphor with which to compare sex because sex *is* the metaphor! So instead of asking, "What parts of life may be compared to sex?" we should ask, "How does sex help us better understand other parts of life?"—especially our discipleship and faithful progression as individuals, couples, and parents.

Chapter Highlights

While behaviors are an important part of the law of chastity, they are not the heart of the law. Charity and virtue are at the heart of the law, thus making it more of a spiritual issue that should first be embraced in our hearts and our minds before it is expressed in our behaviors.

Young adults reflecting back on their growing up experiences repeatedly say that they wish their parents and leaders had simply talked to them openly—and thoroughly—about sex. Rather than using object lessons to "talk about sex without talking about sex," parents should focus on building relationships with their children that foster open, responsive conversation.

Thought Questions

Which metaphor best describes how you learned about sex while growing up?

As a parent, it is very important to reflect on your own learning experiences and how they influence your current attitudes, feelings, and approaches to sexuality. The first key to raising sexually healthy children is to strive to be a sexually healthy person yourself. Without thoughtful consideration, most parents will simply pass along the style of teaching they experienced while growing up—particularly if they feel awkward or unprepared to discuss sexual matters with their children.

Which metaphor best describes how you are teaching your own children about sex?

If fear, embarrassment, or negative conditioning is influencing your perceptions of sexuality, you will likely use a fear-based approach in your parenting unless you intentionally change your approach. An expansion of your teaching approach will pay great dividends and prepare your children for the intimacies of marriage. Whatever your situation may be, we believe that all lasting change involves three key A's: Awareness, Alternatives, and Action. The remaining chapters in the book will continue to expand your *awareness* of needed change and provide you *alternatives* and specific steps you can take to promote sexual wholeness in your children. As you take *action* with these steps, you'll be well on your way to creating a better way for your children than you had while growing up.

Chapter 2

Moving beyond Abstinence toward Sexual Wholeness

It's hard to get somewhere if you don't know where you are going.

The first steps in understanding healthy sexuality are to embrace the divinely taught vision of sexual wholeness in marriage and to appreciate that human sexual experience is comprised of three primary dimensions: a physical dimension, an emotional dimension, and a spiritual dimension (see figure on opposite page). In the simplest of terms, when these dimensions are unified and in harmony with each other, individuals and couples experience *sexual wholeness*. When the dimensions of our sexuality are not united, we experience *sexual fragmentation*. Let's discuss what sexual wholeness in marriage entails and then lay out how these dimensions form a foundation to draw on as we map out the pathway to sexual wholeness for our children. While we will discuss each of these dimensions as if they were separate and distinct, in reality, they are always intricately intertwined.

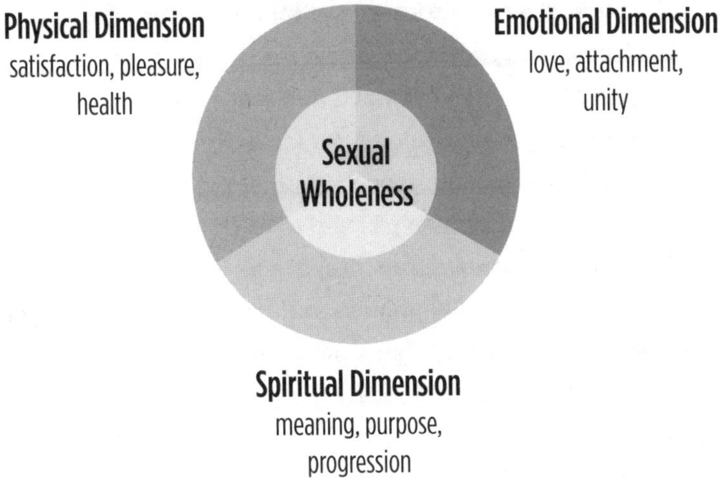

Dimensions of sexual nature.

A Model of Sexual Wholeness in Marriage

The foundations of healthy sexual relationships are developmental in nature and form over time in stages. This is a simple notion that all of us can readily understand. For example, when a young student begins to take dance classes at a studio, she starts with "beginning dance." In time, as she learns the principles and practices of a beginning dancer, she will move on to the "intermediate dance" class and eventually the "advanced dance" class. To develop in life, we have to understand first the beginning stages and then the later stages.

However, there is another way to think about development that involves learning about the peak or optimal stage of development and then working backwards. For example, imagine the prima ballerina of a professional dance company. She is at the pinnacle of dance ability and progression. What was her stage of development right before where she is now? And what about the stage before that, and the stage before that, and so on? Eventually, we can trace a continuous pattern back to the young girl going to the dance studio for the first time.

As parents, we need to have a vision of the final stage or intended goal of sexual wholeness for our children. Complete sexual wholeness is experienced in an eternal marriage where a couple's sexual relationship is tied to God's divine purposes of sexuality. Spouses create true intimacy as they help each other progress in the plan of happiness and interact with each other in ways that meet each other's personal needs. This involves spouses being responsive to each other and seeking out mutually enjoyable experiences that can build their relationship. Complete sexual wholeness in marriage involves three types of bonding or integration—the bonding of the spirit and the body, the bonding of spouses to each other, and the bonding of the couple with God. These three levels of bonding correspond to the three doctrines of human sexuality taught by Elder Jeffrey R. Holland in his landmark talk "Of Souls, Symbols, and Sacraments." Elder Holland emphasized that a sexual union between a man and a woman is intended to be a special and transformative symbol of their relationship: "Human intimacy, that sacred, physical union ordained of God for a married couple, deals with a symbol that demands special sanctity. Such an act of love between a man and a woman is—or certainly was ordained to be—a symbol of their total union: union of their hearts, their hopes, their lives, their love, their family, their future, their everything."[1]

This holistic vision of sexual union in marriage can give us a deeper appreciation for what we want our children to understand about sex. It gives us a vision of helping them become people who can be emotionally responsive to a spouse one day and have a positive attitude about sex and their bodies. It reinforces the importance of helping our children learn to express their sexuality both before and after marriage in ways that are in harmony with God's divine plan for them. It also involves sharing our testimony of the reality of our Savior's Atonement and the blessings of sincere repentance-based growth.

The Three Dimensions of a Child's Sexual Nature

One of the vital truths of the restored gospel is that "the spirit and the body are the soul of man" (D&C 88:15) and that when the spirit and body are separated, men and women "cannot receive a fulness of joy" (D&C 93:34). In this simple truth, we discover a key to help our children avoid the trap of sexual fragmentation and the foundation for helping them eventually develop sexual wholeness in marriage. This doctrine of the soul teaches us that all sexual experiences in this life affect both our bodies and our spirits. It also teaches us that our spirits are the source of our emotions and thoughts, and that in order to have true sexual fulfillment we need to appreciate how they are enmeshed with the physical reactions of our bodies.

The spiritual dimension. We should always remember that our children are spiritual beings having a mortal experience. Because of this, it is in their inherent nature to seek meaning and purpose in their lives. The Proclamation on the Family teaches that each of us "is a beloved spirit son or daughter of heavenly parents, and, as such, each has a divine nature and destiny."[2] Thus, we all have an innate desire to progress. As President Dallin H. Oaks has taught, "Our theology begins with heavenly parents. Our highest aspiration is to be like them."[3] So when we help our children live according to God's will and have faith in His divine plan for them, they will feel contentment and peace because they are filling "the measure of [their] creation" (D&C 88:25). But when our children feel a lack of progression in their lives, that same divine nature gives them feelings or ideas that something is amiss, leaving them to feel restless or frustrated. When such lack of progression results from being out of alignment with God's commandments, they often feel a sense of unworthiness and see a decrease in their faith.

This innate desire to progress is also a part of our children's sexual nature—they all seek for sexual meaning. When our children's sexual expressions are in alignment with God's purposes, they will sense that sex has meaning and purpose in their own lives; it becomes inseparably linked to strong feelings of love for God and for their eventual spouse. This quietly endows them with a sense of worthiness and a growing appreciation for the positive role sex was designed to play in their lives. At times, however, our children will express their sexuality in shallow or meaningless ways that are not in alignment with God's divine purposes for sex. When this happens, their spiritual nature reacts and causes them to feel less content and unfulfilled. We need to help our children recognize the inner promptings they feel related to their sexual development and help them learn more and more each day to follow those promptings and rely on the love and grace of our Savior Jesus Christ.

The physical dimension. The current cultural discussion about human sexuality, in both popular and professional circles, is dominated by the size of body parts, sexual techniques, and products that claim to enhance physical responses. Even sexual desire is seen as emerging from physical origins, as reflected in popular notions of "libido," "sex drive," or "horniness." This has its professional origins in Freud's psychoanalytic theory that viewed humans as having an involuntary, physically-generated sexual energy that must be expressed. The notion of humans having an involuntary, physical sex drive is often used to rationalize inappropriate sexual expression—whether before or during marriage. Such physical-only perspectives fail to include the spiritual and emotional dimensions of our sexual nature, which emphasize the voluntary and controllable capacity for sexual expression and the true human need for love and connectedness. True expressions of love and commitment were never intended to be just one-dimensional manifestations of genes and hormones.

Even though spiritual perspectives caution us to teach our children not to embrace lustful practices that may lead to them focusing on seeking only the physical sensations of their bodies, we should not discount the significance of the physical dimension of our children's sexual nature. Again, Elder Holland's teachings about the doctrine of the soul help us see that our physical bodies are essential to our happiness. In fact, one of the major purposes of this life is for the spirit children of God to receive physical bodies, and we know that after this life, through the power of Christ's Atonement and Resurrection, we can live like our Heavenly Parents—with an immortal physical body. Thus, helping our children live virtuous lives does not mean teaching them to reject the joy of their physical senses; rather, it enlarges their capacity for a full and satisfying enjoyment of them.

The emotional dimension. Each of us has a fundamental need to be deeply connected to others; this is a core part of our divine nature and is shared by all people in all cultures. Elder Bruce C. Hafen explained, "People simply desire to be connected with others, especially in close relationships. They are feeling the longing to belong. . . . Both our theology and the feelings of our hearts make us want to belong, now and eternally, to the father of our Spirits, to his Son, and to those we love on earth."[4] Through the fulfillment of this need we discover genuine security and happiness, as well as lasting motivation to trust, love, and sacrifice for others. Through such belonging and unselfish investment in others, we develop a more complete sense of happiness and well-being.

Our children's innate need for emotional attachment is another part of their sexual nature, and it includes the desire for sexual belonging in a loving couple relationship one day. One of our most important tasks as parents is to help our children learn to appreciate the deep emotional aspects of sex. In contrast with the physical dimension of our children's sexual nature, which gives them the desire for sexual satisfaction, the emotional dimension of their sexual nature provides them with the surprising yet welcome capacity to experience profound fulfillment in the sexual satisfaction they can provide to another person. Their emotional nature makes them relational beings with a capacity for charity and the ability to express true concern for the well-being of others. It is to this part of our natures that Christ was referring when He taught, "He that findeth his life shall lose it: and he that loseth his life for my sake shall find it" (Matthew 10:39). We must help our children learn that true happiness cannot be found in simply satisfying their own desires; it must include meeting the needs of others and fulfilling their need to be loved.

In the remainder of the book we will be sharing ideas for how these three dimensions of a child's sexual nature apply to parenting and how we can better teach our children about their developing sexuality. Again, the goal of our approach is to help our children become sexually whole, which is elevated from the approach of just stopping behaviors and avoiding sins. Parenting from a sexual wholeness perspective helps parents promote *growth rather than guilt* in teaching children about sex. Additionally, parents who begin teaching their children early and often to understand their bodies and talk about these issues can help their children learn to come to them with questions or concerns rather than to hide and repress feelings.

Chapter Highlights

The starting point for healthy sexuality is a testimony of the importance of sexual wholeness in our Father in Heaven's plan and a vision of emulating our Heavenly Parents in the divine institution of marriage.

Healthy sexuality is best understood by appreciating that all sexual experiences are comprised of three primary parts: a physical dimension, an emotional dimension, and a spiritual dimension. When these dimensions are unified and in harmony with each other, we experience sexual wholeness. When they are not, we experience sexual fragmentation.

Parenting from a sexual wholeness perspective helps parents promote growth rather than guilt when teaching their children about sex. This involves creating an open and caring relationship that encourages children to thoughtfully consider their sexual feelings and behaviors and to make choices that will help them express their sexuality in ways that are in harmony with their divine sexual nature.

Thought Questions

How does the ultimate goal of a loving temple marriage help your children understand the divine purposes of sexuality?

How does thinking about the three dimensions of your child's sexual nature help you better teach them the difference between sexual wholeness and sexual fragmentation?

Is there a dimension of sexuality (physical, emotional, or spiritual) you feel you need to work on the most as a parent?

Does your awareness of this one area make you feel guilty or hopeful?

This feeling of guilt or hope may be an indication of whether you approach growth and change through a guilt or growth mentality. It is also likely that you use the same approach with your child.

Putting It into Practice

Questions to start a discussion with your child if you have approached sexuality with too much guilt and not enough growth (adjust as needed for the age of your child):

- I would like to talk with you about how I have approached the topic of sex with you. When you think of your sexual feelings and behaviors, how do you feel about them? Do you feel mostly guilty about them?
- I'm sorry that I have let some of my own guilt about sexuality make you feel guilty. I really want you to know that sexuality is one of the most wonderful gifts of life, and I am going to try to be better at discussing this with you. Do you think we can learn to talk about sex without feeling guilty about it? What do I do or say that makes you feel guilty?

Questions to start a discussion with your child if you have approached sexuality through a growth perspective:

- I appreciate that you have been open with me about your sexual feelings and thoughts. Do you have other questions or concerns that we have not talked about?
- Do you have worries about your sexuality that are hard for you to discuss? How do you feel about yourself spiritually? Do you think your sexual thoughts and behaviors are moving in the right spiritual direction?

Chapter 3

Parents Are Integral

Parenting 101: It's not about the details, it's about the relationship.

Now that we have shared our overarching perspective on the importance of teaching healthy sexuality, let's get down to some specific aspects of parenting that will help pave the way. Because children and youth get messages about sexuality from so many different sources, parents are integral to children's development of healthy sexuality and need to be actively involved in its teaching. Though this might not always feel easy, it is necessary and possible. Elder Larry R. Lawrence reminds us, "Parenting . . . in the latter days is a very humbling assignment. Satan and his followers are striving to bring this generation down; the Lord is counting on valiant parents to bring them up. Parents, 'Be strong and of a good courage; be not afraid.' I know that God hears and will answer your prayers."[1] Parents and children may make mistakes in this process of teaching, but this is a key way that we and they will learn, so we needn't be afraid of mistakes. It is never too late to begin making changes in our relationships.

Curiously, while we are comfortable allowing our children to fall and stub their toes and scrape their knees when they learn to walk, we are less comfortable with the idea of our children making similar mistakes in the sexual area as they learn to direct their maturing bodies and feelings in the proper paths. If we try to protect our children from absolutely every sexual thought, feeling, and potential mistake, we hinder their ability to grow and become self-sufficient in their sexual development. Because of our discomfort regarding sexuality, we often fail to establish the needed lifelong openness with our children around the topic of sexuality, and we make an already challenging transition much harder. Imagine how much more difficult it would be for our babies to learn to walk if they did not have their parents nearby to give them that helping hand as they start to teeter or to pick them up after they fall down and scrape their knee. When we avoid open communication about sexuality with our children, we are essentially making them learn to walk on their own. The guidance and help our children need about their sexuality is no more difficult than reaching out a hand to a toddler who is trying to walk, and we believe that with a little practice, we can start to feel the ease and the necessity of supporting our children through this transition.

To present some general guidelines that will serve as a foundation for the rest of the book, the next two chapters aim to provide us with hope and assurance that we can be the type of parent who has a healthy relationship with our children and can help guide them through sexual development in an appropriate way. This relationship that we have with our children is the key to their hearing and following the principles we hope to instill about sexuality.

Building a Positive Emotional Climate with Your Child

Guideline #1: Start with the parent-child relationship. There is a host of research on parenting, and we couldn't begin to cover it all in this book. That being said, scholars generally distinguish between the emotional climate of the parent-child relationship and the specific strategies parents use to socialize their children. We are all anxious to learn specific things we can do to be better parents, but first and foremost, good parenting is about creating a warm and supportive emotional climate with our children.

When your children think about their relationship with you, do they feel generally supported and loved, while also knowing you have reasonable expectations for them? Or do they feel controlled and dominated, afraid that whatever they say will result in punishment? Or do they feel like you are a friend—that they can talk and joke with you about anything but that you have few expectations for their behavior? If you have no idea how your children would answer these questions, ask them! Or complete the brief questionnaire at the end of this chapter and get an idea for yourself. If we are generally supportive and loving parents who also have reasonable but high expectations for our children, then our parenting style will enable us to help them much more with sexual development—and will also allow us to make more mistakes! A number of child development studies have shown that in the context of a warm emotional climate, specific parenting blunders or mistakes (such as when we totally lose our cool and throw an adult tantrum) are less likely to negatively affect our children. So a positive emotional climate is both a bonus and a buffer; it will open the door to quality discussions about sexuality with children, and it will allow more freedom to be imperfect in the specific parenting practices or strategies used on a day-to-day basis.

In contrast, when we are consistently controlling our children and lack warm interactions with them, it is likely that they will not feel safe talking with us about sexuality and will fear punishment. This approach often leads to shame and secrecy about sexual behaviors, which are more likely to lead to patterns of unhealthy sexual behavior. And, unfortunately, our children's perception of how controlling we are matters more than whether we think we are controlling. The reason children's perceptions of parental control can be so harmful is that if you were to try some of the strategies suggested later in this book, they may fall on deaf ears or be less effective if children feel that you're lecturing or don't have their best interest in mind. We recognize it's no small feat to change the emotional climate of your relationship and that you are not the only person in the relationship. Sometimes a difficult emotional climate is due in large part to the child. However, the most important place to start is in improving the quality of the relationship you currently have so that the specific strategies you try will be more effective.

So how do we as parents improve the emotional climate in our homes in order to allow ourselves the freedom to discuss sexuality with our children and to allow them the comfort to approach us with concerns? This will vary depending on our personal situations and each child's age and temperament, but generally, a positive emotional climate consists of:

1. Reasonable demands for maturity. Do you expect too much of your children? Are you always harping on them because of their mistakes instead of praising them for what they do well? When they make mistakes (including sexual mistakes), do you ask yourself if they did it on purpose or if it was a function of immaturity that comes with an opportunity to learn (and for you to teach)?

2. Set reasonable limits and insist on obedience. Having a positive emotional climate in the home does not mean that your children will always be thrilled with you and that there will be no disagreements. A positive emotional climate is established by clear, consistent, and reasonable expectations, which might also mean a disgruntled child at times. For example, a "no media in the bedroom" rule can be an important safeguard for the development of healthy sexuality, but it may not be popular. Regardless, it should be enforced. It is easiest if you set the rules from an early age; then you will get less pushback when they are teens. But either way, the rules are important and should be enforced!

3. Listen patiently to your child's point of view. When your child comes to you with a sexual concern, do you lecture endlessly, or do you sit down and listen carefully to his or her concerns and worries? You may have much more experience than your children, but establishing a positive emotional climate requires careful listening and an attempt to understand and value them as individuals.

4. Encourage participation in family decision making. When your children make a mistake, do you punish them in a heavy-handed way, or do you allow for discussion and input? When establishing dating rules, for example, do you make it a family discussion, or do you definitively declare what will and will not happen in your home? When you tell your teen that you want a new rule of no media in the bedroom, do you present it as an edict or leave it open for discussion and compromise?

5. Be involved in your children's lives. If your children know you care about them, they will be much more willing to obey you and listen to your counsel about things regarding sexuality. This may mean attending soccer games, band concerts, and dance recitals. It may mean taking the time to sit down individually to discuss concerns or going on "dates" with just you and your child. It means taking the time to be personally invested in each child and his or her developing interests, including sexual interests. Sister Susan W. Tanner said, "We demonstrate our love for family members not only in teaching them affirmatively but also in giving them of our time. . . . A loving relationship requires constant and ongoing talking, playing, laughing, and working moments. We are major players in each other's lives, absorbing love through daily experiences."[2]

When parents take the time to establish a positive emotional climate for their children, it will set the foundation needed to help them learn about healthy sexuality. Parenting research suggests that a positive relationship will increase our children's trust in us and knowledge of our positive intentions. This will lead to a higher likelihood that they will desire to do what we suggest is right and will listen to our wise advice. And remember, one thing at a time. So if you read this list and felt like you needed to work on all aspects of the emotional climate, just pick one and focus on it for a few months. We can't try to run faster than we have strength, or we will just revert to our old habits.

Proactive vs. Reactive Parenting

Guideline #2: Consistent proactive communication is much more effective than sheltering a child against every possible encounter with sexuality. Now that we have established a positive emotional climate, we can get into more specific parenting strategies—or what parents do in specific situations to encourage healthy sexuality. There are two broad types of parenting that are particularly relevant to teaching children heathy sexuality, namely, reactive and proactive parenting. *Reactive parenting* is the most commonly studied, and is how parents respond to a child's misbehavior. So in this case, it would concern how we respond when we find our child has been viewing pornography or masturbating. The behavior has already happened, and we are now reacting. While this aspect of parenting is certainly important, a more imperative aspect is *proactive parenting*, or anticipating the problems children might have and acting before their behavior has become a serious problem. For example, if you notice your child has been watching a television show that depicts permissive sexual behavior, you might suggest finding another show to watch rather than watching the entire series and being influenced by the content. Elder Lawrence provided a helpful reminder of the need for action (and we would say proactive action) when he said, "Imagine for a moment that your daughter was sitting on the railroad tracks and you heard the train whistle blowing. Would you warn her to get off the tracks? Or would you hesitate, worried that she might think you were being overprotective? If she ignored your warning, would you quickly move her to a safe place? Of course you would! Your love for your daughter would override all other considerations. You would value her life more than her temporary goodwill. Challenges and temptations are coming at our teenagers with the speed and power of a freight train. As we are reminded in the family proclamation, parents are responsible for the protection of their children. That means spiritually as well as physically."[3]

Research suggests that most parents wait until they believe their child is sexually active before they talk about sexuality, which is an example of reactive parenting and is akin to waiting until the train has already struck to intervene. According to many of our students, this is a big talk on the night before the child's wedding. However, a proactive approach to healthy sexuality is much more effective than a reactive or avoidant approach. Some of you are in the position where you are reacting to your child's sexual transgression, and you may not have been as proactive as you now realize you could have been. If that is the case, don't feel guilty. Avoid shaming yourself or your child, and start being proactive today. It is actually likely that most of you were and are proactive to some degree, but let's discuss the best ways to be proactive—as well as some ways that are less effective.

There are two main approaches to proactive parenting, namely, cocooning and pre-arming. *Cocooning is a parent's attempt to shelter or protect their children from potentially negative influences*, and is probably an aspect of parenting that is familiar. Naturally, many of us want to shelter our children from pain and suffering. Indeed, research suggests that religious parents are more likely to cocoon than nonreligious parents. In the area of sexuality, cocooning might include sheltering a child from all sexual images, content, and discussions (including thoughts and feelings, as if indeed we could control those in our child!). While it is certainly appropriate to shelter our children from some aspects of sexuality (e.g., installing Internet and television filters), at some point our children are going to be on their own, and the only truly effective filter will be their own self-control. Leading media scholar Amy Nathanson, from Ohio State University, has found that while cocooning is relatively effective for young children, it often backfires on older children and leads to excessive curiosity and the tendency to seek other sources (such as peers or the media) for answers to questions that parents will not address.

In contrast, *pre-arming is defined as parents providing their children with some form of advanced armor against potentially conflicting values messages.* Essentially, it is putting on the whole armor of God: "Wherefore take unto you the whole armour of God, that ye may be able to withstand in the evil day, and having done all, to stand" (Ephesians 6:13). Pre-arming can take many forms and is basically a tool to achieve open communication with children. It means anticipating situations our children might experience and talking with them about how to deal with those situations and feelings. This means that we actually have to think about potential difficult situations our child might encounter regarding sexuality, even if we don't want to!

By way of example, let's say that a parent has a son who is about eleven or twelve. He is starting to develop physically and seems to be more interested in the opposite sex (which is a good thing, so remember to stop and feel happy about this!). He comes to his parent and confesses that he finds himself staring at girls in class and obsessively daydreaming about them, and it is making it difficult for him to concentrate in school. One approach a parent could take would be to install an additional five firewalls on every computer, change the channel every time a Victoria's Secret ad comes on, stand behind the son constantly looking over his shoulder every time he is on the computer, stop allowing him to spend time with female friends, tell him his questions or behaviors are inappropriate, or try to avoid really diving into the issues of sexuality by changing the subject in hopes he will forget about it. Now, some of these examples may be a bit extreme, but be honest: do any of these approaches sound like something you might do? While this cocooning approach will likely protect a child for a time, it will not provide him with the advanced armor he needs to combat our sexually fragmented world and develop healthy sexuality. It might be more comfortable for the parent, but in the long run, it is not what is best for the child.

A more appropriate approach would be for the parent to sit down with the son, give him a big hug (if he will still allow the parent to do that), thank him for being honest, and then listen to his concerns in a nonreactive way. Certainly, maintain the current firewalls you have, keep the computer in a public room, and don't allow him to spend inordinate amounts of time with girls in the absence of adult supervision. But also talk frequently and openly with him and answer all of his questions about his changing body. Give him suggestions of ways he might be able to focus better in class. Help him to realize that his thoughts and feelings are completely normal and wonderful but that they need to be controlled and understood in terms of healthy sexuality and sexuality in marriage.

Also, parents shouldn't assume that because they are proactive, their children will not still struggle with some aspects of sexuality. We believe that a positive emotional climate and a proactive approach will result in fewer struggles, but parents should certainly expect that they'll need to address these issues with children frequently, especially during the teenage years. One of the keys to healthy sexuality is building a relationship of openness with our children and pre-arming them with the tools they will need to develop healthy sexuality. This takes time and diligence and continued desire on the part of the parent (even if the teenage child is seemingly annoyed or unwilling). If we have established a positive emotional climate with our children, as discussed previously, these conversations will be much easier and more effective.

Foster Communication

Guideline #3: Consistent, open communication is more effective than having "the talk." While some of our students tell us that their parents had "the talk" with them at one point or another, we encourage parents to have many, many, many talks with their children about sexuality—one big talk simply isn't enough, and jamming everything into one talk can be counterproductive. If we are proactive and talk with our children about how to behave in situations regarding sexuality, and have helped them to feel comfortable talking with us about sexuality, it is much more likely that they will come to us when they have questions or have committed a sexual transgression, increasing the chances that healthy sexuality will develop and lines of communication will remain open. To be clear, we are not suggesting that parents expose their children to explicit sexual images so that they can talk about how the images make everyone feel. Rather, we are suggesting that you not fast-forward the movie every time someone kisses on screen, and instead use this as an opportunity to talk about the physical, emotional, and spiritual aspects of sexuality to help open lines of communication and begin a process in which the parent becomes the number-one source of information about sexuality (of course, after the movie might be the best time to talk—a surefire way to frustrate our children is to interrupt a movie with a lengthy discussion every time intimacy is portrayed). The car is a great place to have chats about sexuality, as your child can't escape and doesn't have to make eye contact. Talking about sexuality while engaging in yard work or playing a game of catch can also be very effective, especially for children who may not be as accustomed to sitting down and snuggling while chatting. One father we know had a code with his son that whenever his son wanted to talk, he'd ask his dad if they could go and throw the football together. It takes the emphasis off the topic and the child and allows for open communication.

Regardless of where the conversations take place or in what context, we should work hard to avoid attaching fear, discomfort, or disapproval to the topic of sexuality. This, of course, is the opposite of how almost all of us were raised, so it will not be without challenges. However, it is important to remember that we always can and should ask the Lord for help in these struggles. Sister Sharon G. Larsen reminded us, "We are not alone in this sacred trust of parenting, loving, and leading. It is worth every sacrifice, every inconvenient minute, every ounce of patience, personal discipline, and endurance. 'If God be for us, who can be against us?' (Romans 8:31)."[4] We may have some work to do to reduce our anxieties and fears and push ourselves to be courageous enough to share and encourage our children to talk with us regularly about sexuality, but with the help of the Lord, we can do it. With many of our children, curiosity and interest in the topic will emerge very early, almost as soon as they can talk. They will bring up the topic over and over again, and if we will let their comfort with the topic aid us, everything will be easier. Lucia O'Sullivan, professor of psychology at the University of New Brunswick, notes that research on sexual education in schools suggests variable effectiveness, but quality and open parent-child communication about sexuality is effective at helping young people to develop healthy sexuality, especially when a positive emotional environment allows proactive pre-arming tactics to be used effectively.

Chapter Highlights

In the end, it's all about the relationship you have with your child, so this is a very important place to begin. If some of the specific suggestions given throughout the book seem ineffective, you might consider starting with improving your relationship with your child.

Be more proactive and less reactive. Open lines of communication with your child whenever possible. Having a discussion with your child before you think he or she is interested in the opposite sex might be just what you need to do so that your child will come to you when there is something he or she needs to share.

Thought Questions

How did your parents approach sexuality, and how do you feel that influences how you interact with your children?

Do you feel uncomfortable talking with your children about sexuality? If so, what is one thing you could do to try to open lines of communication?

Do you think you are a cocooning parent or a pre-arming parent? If you have predominantly taken cocooning approaches, how can you work to integrate pre-arming more into your interactions with your children?

Do you consistently consult Heavenly Father about the ways in which you parent your children, especially regarding sexuality? If not, how might you more readily include Him?

Putting It into Practice

Install Internet filters and passwords on all devices. Keep computers and handheld devices in a public part of the home; do not allow these devices in bedrooms behind closed doors. Limit the amount of time your child spends with media devices. It is totally acceptable to teach your children self-control by initially helping them set limits.

When a movie or situation with your child's peers elicits a conversation about sexuality, use it as a springboard for discussion. Sometimes children are more willing to talk when it's not directly about them and their behavior.

If you walk through the mall and pass immodest advertisements, use this as an opportunity to talk with your children about modesty and sexuality. Remind your children that the model is a daughter of God with divine worth. Ask your son how he would feel if others were gawking at his sister. Ask your daughter how she thinks that woman felt in that situation in front of the camera and what messages it sends about body image and the worth of women. If your children are super curious and you're feeling brave, you might even use it as an opportunity to discuss the role that lacy underwear or the like can play in the emotional and sexual closeness of a married couple.

Once a week or month start a conversation at the dinner table about something regarding sexuality. You might be surprised when your children start bringing it up!

Make a routine in which you do something special or fun with your child, and use this as an opportunity to see where his or her thinking is about healthy sexuality. Twice a year at the women's session or priesthood session of general conference might be a nice time to establish a routine (such as dinner, dessert, or another outing) and bring this up as one topic. Twice a year isn't enough to have this conversation, but it might be a good time to make sure you have a more in-depth, one-on-one conversation with each child on a regular basis and answer all of his or her questions.

Assess the emotional climate in your home. Consider taking the questionnaire below, or have your children take it on your behalf and then discuss it with your spouse or children.

Set goals in areas you'd like to improve, and get your spouse or children to help you meet those goals.

Emotional Climate Self-Assessment

Answer yes or no to the following statements:

1. I allow my child to give input into family rules.
2. I take my child's desires into account before asking him/her to do something.
3. I explain to my child how I feel about his/her good or bad behavior.
4. I encourage my child to talk about his/her troubles.
5. I emphasize the reasons for rules.
6. I explode in anger toward my child.
7. I threaten to punish my child more than I actually punish him/her.
8. I scold or criticize to try to make my child improve.
9. I use threats as punishments with little or no explanation.
10. I try to make my child feel guilty when he/she does something wrong.

If you answered yes to the first five, you likely have a positive emotional climate with your child. If you answered yes to any of the last five and feel that they happen frequently (especially if you answered no to several of the first five), you might want to consider whether you can improve the emotional relationship with your child as a first step to opening lines of communication. You might also try having your child or spouse answer these for you—it may provide an additional and important perspective.

Chapter 4

Parenting Is Different for Different Children

Why there is no "one size fits all" in parenting.

One of the truly frustrating things about parenting is that just when we think we have it all figured out, we have another child with a new and totally different temperament and personality. Sister Elaine S. Dalton reminded us, "As [children] of God we are each unique and different in our circumstances and experiences."[1] This may mean that many of the fantastic strategies we've mastered with our first child are completely ineffective on our second child. This could be because one of our children is a boy and the other is a girl, or it could be because one of our children is shy while the other is extremely outgoing. Either way, in all the chapters that follow, we encourage parents to tailor their strategies to the particular child with whom they are communicating and consider that what worked for one child might not work for all of them.

Child Age

Throughout this book we refer to developmentally appropriate parenting practices, which signifies how parents respond to children differently at different ages. For example, though you may show your teenager anatomy pictures and discuss sexual arousal, that would not be useful for your three-year-old. Developmental maturity and age are important to consider when deciding how to discuss sexuality with your child. So what do we mean when we say “developmentally appropriate”? Though there are certainly physical developmental milestones we will present throughout the book (especially in Chapter 5), these vary widely by child and are not an indication of emotional readiness or maturity. So in many ways, only you will know what your children are ready for. There is no magical age at which a child is too young or too old to learn about sexuality; it is more important to always be open about sexuality while also varying how to approach the topic. Although we often talk about chronological age, developmental age is a much better gauge of when a child is ready to have some more serious discussions about sexuality. You may have a particularly precocious eight-year-old who has many questions, and you should not deny him or her of this curiosity. Or you may also have a very immature thirteen-year-old who is not quite ready for the timetable you have used with some of your other children and will require a bit of a slower start.

It is worth noting that there are some things parents will always cocoon their child against regardless of age (e.g., pornography), but they might also pre-arm children more as they get older (e.g., actively discuss ways to avoid pornography). The point we are making is that as parents we need to know each child and prayerfully consider how we approach the topic of sexuality.

However, if the topic has been woven into discussions from the time our children were small, there will be much less angst about whether or not we talk; it'll be more about *how* we talk.

One guideline for parents is to follow your child's lead: if he is asking questions or has heard something at school that perplexes him (we are ever amazed at how early our children learn about sex from their peers), it is time for a more detailed conversation. However, sometimes children may need to be pushed to engage in these conversations, even if they are uncomfortable at first. The most frequent question we get from parents is, "When should I start talking with my child about sex, and how do I begin?" The bottom line is that parents should be open to talking with their children about sexuality from the time they are small, but how parents go about doing it will vary as the children become more mature. Thus, try to consider *developmental* age and don't get wrapped up in hard and fast rules about when your child is ready.

Child Temperament

In addition to age, considering a child's temperament is essential to being an effective parent. Temperament includes the biologically based ways in which children respond to the world around them, and it is usually fairly stable over time. Two important temperamental distinctions that have been made by researcher Jerome Kagan, professor emeritus at Harvard University, are children who are *over-regulated* and children who are *under-regulated*. This means that some children have a tendency to control or regulate their emotions and behaviors too much (over-regulated), and other children do not control or regulate their emotions enough (under-regulated). When they are infants, over-regulated children react strongly and negatively in response to loud noises, strong smells, or discomfort, and they may be particularly difficult to sooth. Over time, these children may grow up to be shy, withdrawn, or anxious children and teens. On the other extreme, under-regulated children almost seem to increase their energy and become more engaged when presented with stimuli, but in a positive, active way. As infants these children may be highly active but may also be very laid back. Under-regulated children do not fear authority and grow up to be extroverted and sometimes impulsive children and teens who may be at risk for conduct disorders or risk behaviors.

While these extremes help us to understand temperament, the important thing to remember is that very few children are at the extremes. Because of socialization influences (parenting central among these), most children (about 75%) fall somewhere in between these extremes. As you've been reading, you might have already tried to place your children and their temperamental tendencies in one of these two extremes, but you may have been unsuccessful. Sometimes your son may be anxious or shy, but he can still function and just takes a while to warm up. Your daughter may be excessively energetic and frequently disobedient, but she certainly doesn't have a conduct disorder. What we hope parents can identify from this chapter is your children's overall temperamental *tendencies*, and how these might impact their sexuality and shape your approach to parenting. If you aren't sure already, take the short quiz at the end of this chapter regarding your children's temperaments. While temperament and sexuality are certainly not synonymous, your children's temperamental tendencies will impact how they react to their own developing sexuality.

So how does temperament relate to sexuality? An over-regulated temperament may result in children who are much

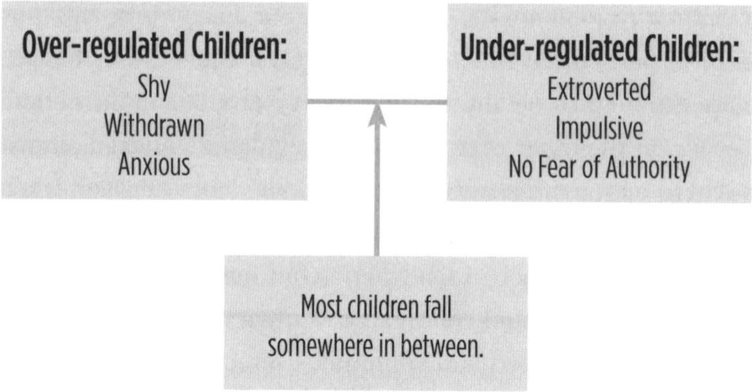

Temperamental profiles that may impact how parents talk about sexuality.

more anxious and reserved about sexuality, who are prone to shame and repression when they have sexual feelings. On the other hand, an under-regulated temperament may result in an individual who has trouble regulating sexual feelings and behaviors and may be more prone to struggles with flirting and wanting to date at early ages. These tendencies should impact how we parent our children. Research from our lab has found that when considering sexuality in particular, about 31% of females are considered over-regulated, 16% under-regulated, and just over 50% somewhere in the middle, while 20% of males are considered over-regulated, 35% under-regulated, and just under 50% fall in the middle. This tells us a few important things.

First, most of our children are probably pretty balanced sexually, and thus most of the suggestions we made in the prior chapter will work just fine, with some minor tweaking here or there. However, a sizable portion of our sons may struggle with under-regulated sexuality (many of us probably would have guessed higher, so maybe the eye-opener is that it's only 35%), while a relatively equal number of our daughters struggle with over-regulated sexuality. It is also of note that almost 20% of males and females are what we'd consider to be slightly against stereotype (over-regulated for boys and under-regulated for girls), which is important to consider. If we follow stereotype and assume our daughters are not at all sexual and our boys are hypersexual, we may miss the opportunity to parent these children to the best of our ability. So what can we do as parents to alter our approach for different children?

For children with a tendency to be over-regulated. If parents are cocooning and noncommunicative or punishing about sexuality, over-regulated children will be much more stressed, feel more shamed, and likely develop less healthy sexuality than would the average child—in other words, they may be more negatively impacted by parenting mistakes. The good news is that children at these extremes also benefit more from appropriate parenting, so take heart. It may take a bit more effort for children who are over-regulated to open up regarding sexuality, and parents may spend quite a bit of time wondering what is going on inside their heads. Keep at it! Don't shut down just because your child seemingly doesn't want to talk about it. Again, if you've started opening lines of communication early, this won't be as much of a challenge, but some children just don't seem to want to talk no matter how much a parent has prepped them. One tactic that we have found to be effective is having conversations with a child who is over-regulated and also with a sibling who is under-regulated at the same time. This allows the extroverted and chatty child to ask all the questions and the over-regulated child, who really wants to talk about it but doesn't know how, to still get all the great answers and maybe even pluck up the courage to ask a question or two.

Children who are over-regulated will be at much greater

risk of fear, shame, and secrecy, so parents should be especially careful not to attach punishment with sexual behavior if their child is of this persuasion. But remember, just because an over-regulated child is not acting out sexually does not mean that he or she has healthy sexuality! If over-regulated children are struggling with sexuality, they are much more likely to be doing so in secret, and it therefore may be harder for you to pick up on. Grazyna Kochanska, professor of developmental psychology at the University of Warsaw, suggests that parenting strategies such as setting limits and appropriate rules are quite effective for over-regulated children (as they are unlikely to push back), so you might need to keep yourself from overly cocooning children with this temperamental tendency because they may be more willing to be sheltered than would children who are under-regulated. Gentle discipline is much more effective with children who are over-regulated than is harsh discipline, because even a slight raise of the voice is experienced as painful and punishing. So parents should be gentle when over-regulated children make sexual mistakes and be patient as they try to encourage them to share their feelings. These children may especially benefit from distraction or activity while discussing sexuality or prefer being in a situation where eye contact isn't necessary. They will likely have numerous questions about their growing and changing bodies but will not be as well equipped to give voice to those questions and may be more prone to trying to find answers in private, so be sure to check in frequently. Sometimes the quiet and unassuming children get unintentionally ignored simply because they aren't the squeaky wheel—so it is our job as parents to go out of our way to engage children with these temperaments.

For children with a tendency to be under-regulated. In

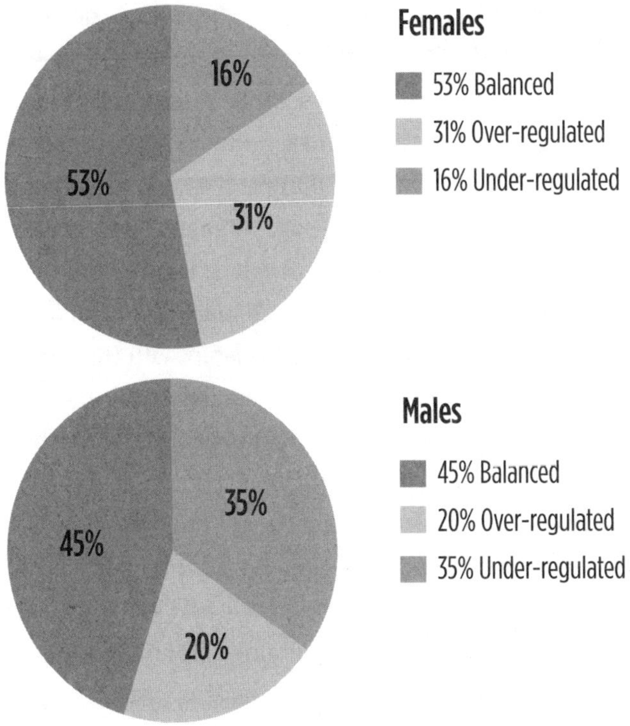

Temperamental approaches to sexuality by gender.

contrast, parents likely will have no problems getting children who are under-regulated to ask questions and talk about sexuality, but helping them to control their behavior may be more of a challenge. Parents need to start by acknowledging that their children are not flawed or shameful in any way but that temperamental tendencies will make this part of development (and probably others) a bit more difficult to manage. Parents with children in this camp will likely feel this is a bigger problem than over-regulation because it is external and noticeable, but we challenge this notion. In some ways, it is easier to identify a problem with an under-regulated child and then help to solve it because it's often all out in the open. Under-regulated children often don't respond particularly well to discipline (because they more rarely experience anxiety or fear of punishment), but they do tend to respond well to the positive emotional climate discussed in Chapter 3, as it creates a bond and a feeling that they can trust and depend on their parent. If they feel this security, they will often have a greater desire to adhere to parental rules and eventually internalize parental values as their own in an attempt to make their parents happy and maintain the relationship. This will then transfer to their relationship with their Heavenly Father, as Elder Dieter F. Uchtdorf reminds us, "We increase our love for our Heavenly Father and demonstrate that love by aligning our thoughts and actions with God's word. His pure love directs and encourages us to become more pure and holy."[2]

Under-regulated children respond particularly well to parenting practices that include pre-arming and joint conversation and decision making (especially about potential consequences to others) regarding possible transgressions. So parents shouldn't harshly punish under-regulated children, even though they may consistently make mistakes. If we punish and shame, they will just begin to be more secretive and become more likely to develop long-term problems. Instead, we need to provide specific strategies and safeguards for these children to use when feeling tempted or lacking in control. Help them to feel the love and patience that the Savior feels for all of us when we are going through the process of repentance, especially when it comes to sin or transgression that is repeated and difficult to overcome. We need to provide encouragement and let our children know that they are not alone in this struggle.

The bottom line is that one size does not fit all children when it comes to parenting, and this is no exception when we are teaching our children about sexuality. The first positive step is to notice and acknowledge the differences in our children and stop trying to fit a square peg into a round hole. The best parent is a flexible parent, so be willing to try something new and to not treat your children the same, all the "it's not fair" lectures from your children notwithstanding. Because the point here is our children are *not* the same, and they may require a different tactic depending on their experiences, gender, age, temperament, or all of the above.

Sexual Safety

A specific topic that should be proactively discussed with children but will vary depending on the child's age and temperament is sexual safety. From the time children are very young, before they start elementary school, it is important to teach them about sexual safety, such as what is safe touch and what is unsafe touch that might occur between friends or between adults and children. As children grow older, this sexual safety discussion should expand to include how to help children avoid sexual predators online and elsewhere. Care should also be taken to tailor the discussion of sexual safety for children of different temperaments. For example, over-regulated children might become very frightened if parents are too graphic about sexual safety too soon, while under-regulated children might not be frightened enough. Being sensitive to a child's temperament doesn't mean putting off a necessary conversation, but it might mean softening the message or introducing ideas gradually.

While it is beyond the scope of this book to thoroughly cover sexual safety, there are some resources at the end of this chapter that you might find useful. We recommend that you discuss sexual safety at least annually with your children. But, importantly, *never combine a discussion of sexual safety and healthy sexuality in the same conversation.* Usually children will feel some appropriate sense of anxiety and fear during discussions about sexual safety, and it is a topic that naturally has some fear associated with it. However, it is not helpful to connect fear with healthy sexuality, and this is a common error many parents and leaders have made over the years that is very difficult to untangle, even after people are married. Fear and anxiety are the quickest ways to damage healthy sexual expression. We don't want to help our children be chaste using a fear-based approach by talking about all of the bad things that can happen to them like diseases, pregnancies, etc. We want to encourage and guide them to be chaste by helping them focus on the positive rewards of chastity and the goals they have for their lives like wanting to have the best marriage and family life possible.

Chapter Highlights

There is no magical age at which your child is too young or too old to learn about sexuality; instead, it is about always being open with your child about sexuality while also varying how you approach the topic at your child's different ages.

Different children may have very different temperaments that necessitate discussing sexuality in different ways that are sensitive to each child's individual needs. In this case, the best thing you can do, the most fair thing, is to know your children well enough to treat them differently—according to what will work best for each of them.

It is important to discuss sexual safety regularly, but avoid pairing discussions about sexual safety with discussions about healthy sexuality.

Resources for Parents to Consider for Promoting Sexual Safety

Your role in preventing sexual assault:

- https://rainn.org/articles/your-role-preventing-sexual-assault

Sexual abuse warning signs:

- http://www.parentsprotect.co.uk/warning_signs.htm

Protecting younger children from sexual abuse:

- https://www.care.com/a/7-tips-for-talking-to-kids-about-sexual-abuse-1204090143
- http://www.huffingtonpost.com/mary-1-pulido-phd/talking-to-your-child-about-sexual-abuse_b_3581232.html

Sexual abuse and teenagers:

- http://www.sparksummit.com/

Internet safety:

- http://savvycyberkids.org/default.aspx
- https://support.apple.com/en-us/HT201304
- http://ikeepsafe.org/parents/
- https://netsanity.net/
- https://safesmartsocial.com/teen-apps-digital-citizenship-conference/

Sexual abuse in schools:

- http://stopsexualassaultinschools.org/

Steps you can take to prevent sexual assault:

- https://rainn.org/articles/steps-you-can-take-prevent-sexual-assault

Healing from sexual abuse:

- http://www.peacefulheartsfoundation.org/
- https://rainn.org/recovering-sexual-violence
- http://www.uhs.wisc.edu/assault/recovery.shtml

Books:

- *I Said No! A Kid-to-Kid Guide for Keeping Private Parts Private*, by Valerie and Zack King

- *NO Trespassing: This Is MY Body!*, by Patti Fitzgerald
- *The Right Touch: A Read-Aloud Story to Prevent Child Sexual Abuse*, by Sandy Klevenand Jody Bergsma
- *The Body Keeps the Score: Brain, Mind, and Body in the Healing of Trauma*, by Bessel van der Kolk, MD
- *The Courage to Heal: A Guide for Women Survivors of Child Sexual Abuse*, by Ellen Bass and Laura Davis
- *The Right to Innocence: Healing the Trauma of Childhood Sexual Abuse*, by Beverly Engel
- *The Well-Armored Child: A Parent's Guide to Preventing Sexual Abuse*, by Joelle Casteix

Thought Questions

Has the way you discuss sexuality changed from when your children were younger? If not, what change could you make?

What type of temperament do you have (under-regulated, over-regulated, or somewhere in between)? How has this influenced your sexuality and your parenting?

How does your own temperament interact with the temperament of your child? Is it harder for you to talk with your child because you're over-regulated and she is under-regulated? How might you and your spouse overcome any temperamental mismatch?

How can an understanding of divine nature and individuality, coupled with continued counsel with Heavenly Father, better help you to understand your unique child?

Putting It into Practice

Have a family conversation about sexuality, both with younger children and older children. This will allow your younger children to ask questions and your older children to answer. We have found that sometimes our children know more than we give them credit for, and if we allow them to teach, we may find out a lot. Siblings are often a key source of information about sexuality, so try using this to your advantage!

Give your children (or complete for your children) the survey on the next page to see if they are more under- or over-regulated. If you're feeling very open, have every member of the family fill it out and discuss together what the results might mean for each individual family member's sexuality. This measure is most appropriate for children ages ten and above, but it will give you a good idea of your children's temperament at any age.

If your children tend to be over-regulated, try finding unique ways to engage them in conversations about sexuality where they might not have to be so center stage. For example, have your children anonymously write down questions about sexuality in a jar and pick one out and discuss it each week. Or have a family home evening on sexuality and then play a game in which your children answer questions and ask questions.

If your children are under-regulated, brainstorm ideas with them for how they can better distract themselves and avoid triggers. Of course, reminding your children that these feelings are natural and normal and discussing the deep meaning of sexuality is helpful and necessary, but sometimes good old-fashioned distraction works wonders. Ideas for distraction include a song or chant that will help refocus inappropriate thoughts, a bracelet or ring that will remind them to make good choices, a favorite scripture or conference talk they can turn to in moments of temptation, or places and activities they should avoid, such as surfing the Internet with no purpose, having excessive free time, or using media late at night. Also provide your children with questions they can ask themselves if they come across pornography or start to fixate sexually on an individual.

These questions will help make the objectified individual a "person": (e.g., "I wonder what his favorite color is," "I wonder what she likes to do with her family," "How would he feel if he knew I was sexualizing him instead of respecting him?"). Giving others personhood helps us to think of them as human beings and not objects and can contribute to healthy patterns of sexuality.

Child Temperament Assessment

1. Does your child act uncomfortable around new people?
2. Does your child become nervous or agitated in unfamiliar situations?
3. Is your child reluctant to try new things?
4. Does your child get embarrassed easily?
5. Does your child get anxious when in front of people (e.g., spelling bee, performance, giving a lesson or talk)?
6. Does your child have a hard time sitting still for long periods of time (e.g., at movies, church, school)?
7. Does your child struggle to control his or her strong negative emotions (e.g., have angry outbursts)?
8. Does your child express positive emotions inappropriately (e.g., extensive giggling in a sad situation)?
9. Does your child have a hard time resisting temptation when told not to do something?
10. Does your child have a hard time stopping an activity when it is time to be finished?

If you answered yes to most of the first five items, then your child is more over-regulated. If you answered yes to most of the last five items, your child is more under-regulated. If your yes and no responses were relatively equal within each group of five items, your child is temperamentally somewhere in between (or balanced).

SECTION 2

HELPING YOUR CHILD UNDERSTAND THE PHYSICAL BODY

Chapter 5

Basics of Sexual Anatomy and Puberty

Why handing your child a "what's happening to my body book" isn't enough.

So far we have introduced you to our approach to healthy sexuality, given you a brief introduction to the three aspects of sexual wholeness (physical, emotional, and spiritual), and shared some practical advice and foundational knowledge. The following chapters will become more and more specific and will combine research and gospel truths to provide you with some very important information about your children and some specific suggestions you might use while trying to teach healthy sexuality. This information is crucial for educating your children and providing you and them with the language and information you need to base your sexuality discussions on accurate information rather than on prohibitions and fear. In the next four chapters, we will provide information on normal maturation, puberty, body image, and modesty as they relate to sexual wholeness. This will set a solid foundation for the final chapters, wherein we construct more specific understanding of difficult issues.

Sexual Beings

Understanding the basics of sexual development is particularly important because we are all sexual beings from the moment of conception. As a result of children constantly seeking to learn, even very young children tune in to attitudes and ideas about their bodies and sexuality. How we refer to body parts (using the correct name for each part), the tone of voice we use when talking about our body (positive and upbeat), how we respond to children's natural curiosity about their own bodies (always encouraging them to understand how their body works), and even our attitude about our own bodies (presenting happy, healthy, satisfied assessments of our own bodies) will contribute to how our children view their sexuality. Young children want to know about their bodies and others' bodies—this is their natural curiosity. They may touch their own genitals or attempt to see others while they're naked or undressing. This typical behavior is most often a child's effort to explore his or her body and the feelings that are evoked by touching it. If you have young children and openly give accurate information, their curiosity will be satisfied, they will understand the feelings they're experiencing, and they will be empowered to better understand their own sexual development. We are all too happy to marvel at our children's ten fingers and toes, their eyes, ears, mouth, and nose. Why not also teach our children the glorious abilities of their penis or vagina (in developmentally appropriate ways, of course)? We can explain that this new experience of having a physical body is a blessing and an adventure. It is so fun to have a body!

Young Children

Some parents might wonder if it is normal for their two-year-old to play with his penis and anus (or her vagina). Two-year-olds are naturally curious about their bodies. The reality that his penis gets bigger, or erect, when he touches it is also just the normal workings of his body. We know from experience and research that children at this age are very tactile—they learn from touch. A child touching his or her anus indicates a child who is making an effort to really understand his or her body. Children are simply exploring the incredible bodies they have been given. Parents can give the message that mortality is quite an adventure and that understanding our bodies is a part of that adventure. If you feel the need to discourage sexual touch at this age, distraction is the best approach, and shaming should not occur (for more on self-touching, see Chapter 9). The bottom line for younger children is that physical exploration is normal and is in no way an indication that your child will have any issues with sexuality in the future. One of our students told a story about asking her three-year-old son what his favorite body part was. He gleefully replied, "My penis!" The response should be, yes, a penis is a wonderful body part and something to be excited about.

Early and middle childhood are sometimes considered a time of sexual latency, when sexual feelings are not quite as strong. However, research suggests that development is continuing in all areas for our children during this phase, including sexual development. You may be surprised how early your son or daughter starts developing in a sexually noticeable way, and puberty is beginning earlier and earlier, especially for girls in industrialized nations. The bottom line is that it is normal for our young children to be interested in their bodies, and this natural curiosity, if dealt with openly by parents (more on this in Chapter 6), will help when more noticeable physical changes begin in the teen years.

Teenagers and the Physical Consequences of Puberty

Let's begin this section with an example: Yolanda's son Marcus is thirteen years old and in the eighth grade. He seems less willing to talk openly than he was when he was younger, and he spends more and more time in his room alone, listening to music. He has always seemed younger than his friends, and Yolanda's not sure if he's curious about girls or not—he never *seems* to talk about them or to be interested. However, she's noticed him sneaking peaks at advertisements of women in the mall, and at church he is constantly glancing around and lingering after classes as if looking for a certain someone. Last summer Marcus had a big growth spurt, started growing armpit hair, and now looks like he might be getting a mustache. Yolanda is wondering if he has had his first wet dream or has experimented with masturbation, but she isn't sure how to talk to him about it without embarrassing him and herself. She thinks maybe her husband should just talk to him, but he and Marcus don't have a very good relationship. So far she has just ignored the reality that is staring her in the face, but she continues to feel Marcus pull away and worries that he might be involved in behaviors that she could better help him understand. How can she help him to see that his development is normal and wonderful, and while it needs to be kept within boundaries, it should also be reason for celebration?

This situation, or a similar one for young women experiencing their first menstrual period, might be familiar for you as a parent. We acknowledge the struggle that it is to find the right words to discuss developing sexuality with your children and the struggle that adolescent children are facing as they strive to do what's right amidst the hormonal and physical changes of puberty. Although Marcus's development was relatively normal, many girls and boys are starting puberty even earlier, with some young women beginning puberty as early as seven years old (in general, girls start puberty two years earlier than do boys). This example highlights the need to talk with children about puberty and sexuality at an early age, though we acknowledge how difficult this might be for parents. Research suggests that when children know about puberty and what is happening to their bodies, the changes that take place are a much more positive experience than when they have no idea what is happening to them. Every semester we hear anecdotal stories from our students about how they didn't know what was happening to their bodies and how scary it was, which is a stark contrast to those youth who were prepared and supported throughout the physical changes of puberty. Female students are generally much more open about this than are male students—maybe because parents are even less likely to talk with their sons about puberty than they are their daughters. But boys need this type of discussion and openness as much as girls.

Once children approach the teen years, sexual development generally occurs in a natural sequence (see the following charts). For boys, the sequence typically begins with the enlargement of the scrotum and testes, lengthening of the penis (between eleven and thirteen years old), and enlargement of seminal vesicles and prostate glands. This is generally followed by growth of pubic hair, growth of facial and underarm hair (about two years after growth of pubic hair), and the potential for ejaculation (between twelve and fourteen years old). Boys may also experience a growth spurt during this time frame, and typically their voice deepens. Parents may notice a change in their teenager's emotions and behavior prior to the onset of sexual development. For boys, emotional changes can range from greater feelings of aggression to more interest in girls. They may also want to establish greater independence. Additionally, young boys may need more sleep because of this rapid physical and emotional development.

For girls, the sequence typically begins somewhat earlier than for boys. Young girls can begin anytime from eight to ten years old to have vaginal discharge (can range in color from clear to slightly milky-white colored). Vaginal discharge is quite normal and serves important functions, including cleaning and carrying away bacteria and dead cells from the vagina and cervix. About the same time, girls may begin to experience breast budding, and their breasts may be sensitive to touch. About two years after these developments, girls will begin to grow pubic hair and soon after will experience menarche, or their first period. Then, about two years after menarche, underarm hair will grow, and finally, fully developed breast size is apparent. Although the order of maturation is typically standard (though variations certainly occur), the onset of maturation may widely vary. So, although many girls may begin developing between eight to ten years old, others may do so later or earlier (see Chapter 6 for more on puberty). Girls may experience heightened emotions as well. It is a good time to help both young men and young women talk more about their emotions and gain some skills in identifying and describing how they feel.

Teenagers and the Social Consequences of Puberty

Puberty begins as a result of hormones that are released

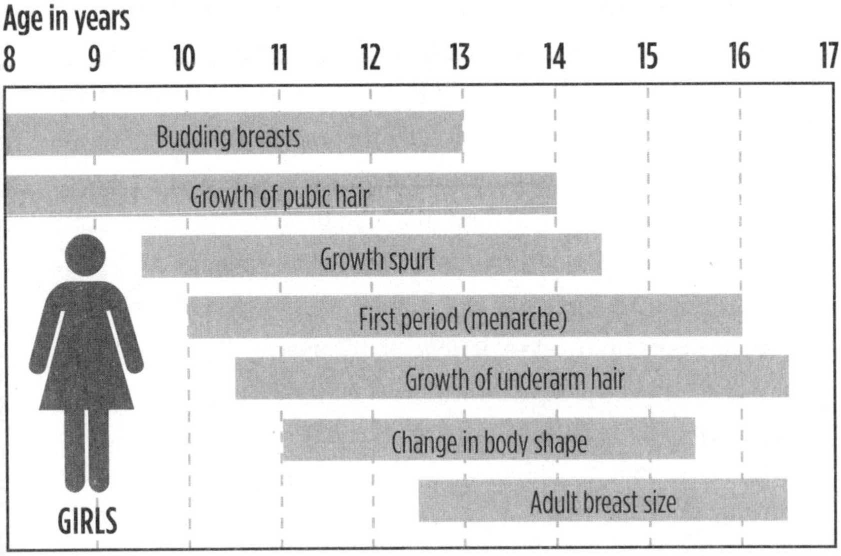

Age in years
8
9
10
11
12
13
14
15
16
17
Budding breasts
Growth of pubic hair
Growth spurt
First period (menarche)
Growth of underarm hair
Change in body shape
Adult breast size
GIRLS

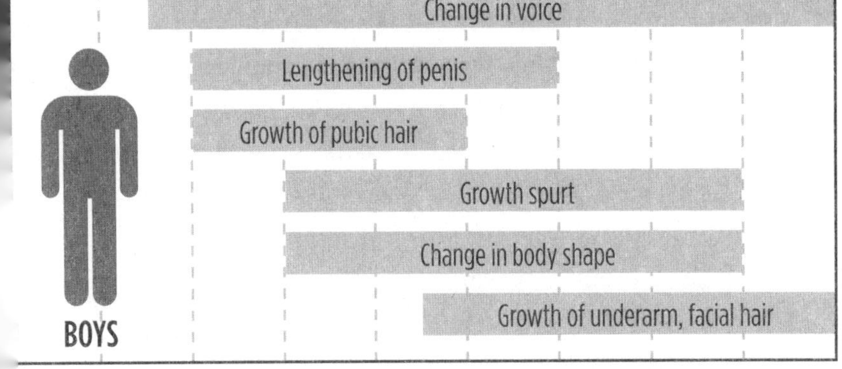

Age in years
9
10
11
12
13
14
15
16
17
18
Growth of scrotum and testes
Change in voice
Lengthening of penis
Growth of pubic hair
Growth spurt
Change in body shape
Growth of underarm, facial hair
BOYS

into the body and send "messages" to the cells alerting the body that it is time to get ready for childbearing (some call it the "puberty alarm"). Though some aspects of pubertal timing are genetic, for females in particular, the onset of puberty is also influenced by proteins contained in fat cells. One of the reasons females mature earlier than males is because they generally have higher levels of body fat, which also explains why girls who are heavier begin puberty earlier, while girls who have very low levels of body fat experience later onset of puberty. There are also ethnic differences, with Hispanic and African-American girls typically beginning puberty earlier than do Caucasian or Asian girls. Family influences—in particular, stressful family environments—can also impact the release of hormones and the start of puberty, with small to moderate levels of stress influencing early onset of puberty and excessive amounts of stress tending to slow maturation. This is an important reminder of just how important the family environment is for our children, even with something as biologically based as puberty.

Pubertal status is an indication of what is physically occurring for children, but *pubertal timing* (or when teens begin developing in comparison to their peers) is usually a much more salient aspect of development for children and can have some pretty serious emotional effects. If parents are aware of these effects and discuss them with children, the process tends to go more smoothly. Early-maturing teens are those who develop earlier than their peers, while late-maturing teens develop later than their peers. The effects of pubertal timing, however, vary for girls and boys (and for individual children, so remember that when we report research findings, we are just reporting norms—your child may be different).

W. Andrew Collins (professor emeritus, Stanford University)

and Laurence Steinberg (professor, Temple University) write about early and late maturation during adolescence in the *Handbook of Child Psychology*. These researchers suggest that early-maturing girls are at the highest risk of all groups, as they often are heavier than their peers and may suffer from self-esteem and body image issues, which can have long-term effects on the development of healthy sexuality. Early-maturing girls also are more likely to become involved in early sexual behavior and other risky behavior, likely because they look older than they are and therefore get more attention from older boys. Early-maturing boys, on the other hand, tend to experience an increase in popularity and self-esteem because they are the biggest and strongest of their age group, but they are also more likely to be involved in early risk behaviors (e.g., drinking and drug use) and are often expected to be more mature than they are mentally ready to be. Early-maturing boys are also at risk for early sexual debut, which again can have a long-lasting impact on the development of healthy patterns of sexuality. Both early-maturing girls and boys are maturing physically faster than they are developing impulse control (which is the last part of the brain to develop and is still maturing into the early twenties). This may result in higher levels of sexual experimentation or more mistakes in this area that will require extra patience and understanding.

Late maturation compared to peers is a very different situation with different outcomes. This can be difficult because no teenager likes to be different and be teased for still looking like a little kid. In contrast to early-maturing girls who may be strapping down their large breasts, late-maturing girls might be stuffing the bras that they do not even need! However, because these girls are usually thin and have lower body fat, the negative effects of late maturation are generally lessened once they hit puberty, and late maturation also protects girls from early sexual involvement. Late-maturing males, on the other hand, are at slightly greater risk of ridicule and self-esteem problems because they often struggle with athletic prowess and may be picked on continually by their peers. Because our society places so much emphasis on male strength and athleticism, it is often difficult for late-maturing boys to find other activities that help to build self-esteem, and they may find it challenging to avoid ridicule from peers for being short or small or, in some cases, overweight. Sometimes these years of teasing by peers have a long-lasting impact on how boys feel about their bodies, which may impact sexuality and confidence during marriage.

Again, your child may be an exception to the patterns of pubertal timing that have been found in research, but it is important to understand which group your child may be in (early- or late-maturing—or on time with peers) and think about how that might be impacting your child's social development. Certainly parents and siblings should avoid teasing a child who might be sensitive about her growing breasts or his short stature. If the home can be a place where your child feels accepted and understood, and where he or she can talk openly about concerns and questions, many of the negative potential outcomes of pubertal timing can be avoided—and puberty can be a part of healthy sexual development (see Chapter 7 for more discussion of how parents can help promote positive body image).

Teenagers and the Emotional Consequences of Puberty

In addition to physical and social aspects of maturation, during adolescence children are experiencing a number of emotional changes that impact sexuality. In particular, sexual arousal (which is not just physical but emotional, too) is new to adolescents, but *explaining* sexual arousal is probably new to most parents. The potential for sexual arousal is planted in each of us. *Learning how to appropriately regulate that sexual arousal is essential for healthy sexual development.* Think of toddlers who are flooded with new, overwhelming emotions and regularly end up in a crying fit because they lack appropriate emotional regulation. The two extremes of *emotional arousal* are children who are too easily excited by new experiences on one side and children who lack enthusiasm for any new experience on the other.

We can see parallels with our adolescents' sexual arousal. We see adolescents who are overwhelmed by the new experiences of sexual arousal and others who may lack enthusiasm for this new development in their life. The ideal adolescent would be excited to discover this aspect of his or her nature and accept guidance from parents to learn how to regulate this arousal. Much of how our children respond to these new feelings is tied to how *we* respond to these feelings. Are we excited for this next step in their life, or do we dread it, try to suppress it, or make jokes about it? One way to facilitate healthy sexual regulation during maturation is to discuss with your children the normal arousal patterns they experience on a daily basis and how those arousal levels can be used to guide their thoughts and behavior. This is likely new territory for parents as well. Regular talks will help parents to develop better explanations and will allow children time to formulate questions as they arise.

You might ask, "What exactly is arousal?" Arousal is simply a stirring to behavior. The word *arousal* is often only associated with sexual feelings, but many examples outside of sex can help us to understand that arousal comes in many forms. We may feel emotional arousal when we see a beautiful piece of art—we are moved by the heightened emotion of the scene. We may feel intellectual arousal after a particularly thoughtful conversation with friends—we are moved to deeper thought and reasoning. A spiritual arousal is explained in the scriptures repeatedly as a need to "arouse the faculties of your souls," (Jacob 3:11; see also Alma 32:27)—a motivation to live closer to the Spirit. In LDS culture, we are often hesitant to use the term *arousal* because of its association with sexual arousal. However, it is helpful to discuss and understand the nuanced gradations of arousal. While emotional, spiritual, physical, and intellectual arousal can begin with similar feelings—and each type of arousal moves us toward a type of behavior—sexual arousal moves us toward sexual behavior, which has a steeper pattern of arousal leading to sexual climax or orgasm. Sometimes it is difficult in the early phases of arousal to distinguish between emotional, spiritual, physical, or intellectual arousal and sexual arousal, especially if arousal has not been openly discussed.

Ideally, we would talk with our children about how sexual arousal is normal and that by paying close attention to how their bodies work and feel, they can better understand when this arousal is moving them toward sexual behavior. Giving our children the room to think and talk about arousal will create a considerable difference in how well they understand their bodies. We need to teach our children to not judge their sexual feelings, but to be aware of them. These are godly feelings. But while these are godly feelings, feelings of arousal also need to be regulated. By talking to our children about their arousal and what may trigger sexual arousal, we will help them understand where *their* boundaries should be to maintain the guidelines Heavenly Father has given.

Very few people understand themselves without some practice. So this process of understanding sexual feelings takes some trial and error. Parents' open invitation for discussion gives their children opportunities to work at understanding these new feelings within safe boundaries. An example of how individuals may need different boundaries can be seen in the commandment to abstain from premarital sex. For some youth, refraining from heavy kissing or touching private areas of the body maintains safety—and that is the guideline that our leaders have given. Others may recognize that they are stirred to sexual behavior by even a lingering hug or some types of dancing. What is most helpful is creating an open environment where your children can talk openly about what *their* feelings are, what sexually arouses *them* and what *they* should avoid.

Elder Jörg Klebingat of the Seventy warned us of an often-used tactic of Satan: "Whenever the adversary cannot persuade imperfect yet striving Saints such as you to abandon your belief in a personal and loving God, he employs a vicious campaign to put as much distance as possible between you and God."[1] Satan engages in a distortion campaign with our sexual identities. Our sexual nature is divine and brings us closer to God. So Satan's attacks on sexuality have been twofold: to make sexual sin seem acceptable or to desexualize us and convince us to deny or minimize the importance of our own sexuality. Neither indulging our sexual feelings nor eliminating our sexual feelings is appropriate. In reality, some individuals may bounce between these extremes, sometimes indulging sexual feelings and then trying to deny their sexuality. The only healthy approach is to acknowledge the divinity of our sexual nature, work to understand and appropriately regulate our sexual thoughts and

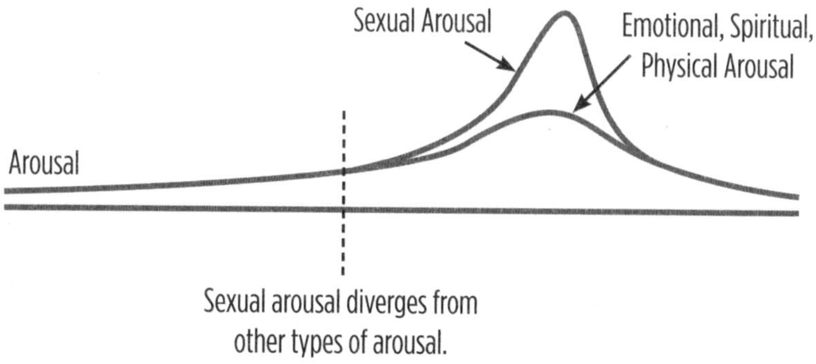

arousal, and always recognize that the source of these sacred embers of sexual feelings is the Giver of Life.

Taken together, the physical, social, and emotional changes that take place in our children over time are natural and normal, and understanding these changes can help us to more easily discuss them with our children, which is the focus of the next chapter.

Chapter Highlights

Sexual development occurs in a natural sequence. For girls, it can begin as early as eight or nine years old; for boys around ten or eleven years old. Development takes a few years and includes social, emotional, and physical changes. Parents who can talk openly about these changes will make this transition easier for their children.

During these years of physical sexual development, children experience heightened sexual arousal and need to learn to regulate their arousal. Talking about how our bodies work and the natural patterns of arousal will help children understand how to better appreciate and regulate this beautiful part of who they are.

Thought Questions

How did your parents respond to your puberty experience, and how has that influenced how you feel about puberty and its role in your spiritual and sexual development?

What can you do to prepare your children for the physical, social, and emotional changes they will experience during puberty?

Is arousal included in your discussions on sexuality? What are the arousal patterns your child faces? Are your children comfortable talking about these patterns?

Putting It into Practice

Have a discussion about how a baby is conceived. This discussion could include regularly reflecting on how complex and joyful this process is and how wonderful it is that Heavenly Father created a process for children to come into the world.

Begin a conversation about emotional or intellectual arousal. Encourage the conversation to include sexual arousal and how it may be different from other types of arousal.

Once talking about sexual development is a comfortable and regular part of your relationship with your children, have a question-and-answer session with them. If you are unsure of the answer to any of their questions, tell them you are not sure but will research their question and get back to them with an answer.

Chapter 6

Discussing and Celebrating Puberty

Just call it like it is! Why avoiding cute names for body parts is a good start.

A father and mother have three children: Katy, 14; Ethan, 10; and Jacob, 2. The parents have felt uneasy talking about the details of maturation, and to this point they have avoided doing so. Katy developed breasts and started her period without her parents preparing her for the experience beyond a very brief talk about her "time of the month" and handing her a box of maxi pads. She'd had to ask her mom to buy her a bra because she was embarrassed when a boy pointed out that her nipples were showing through her T-shirt. She was too embarrassed to talk with her mother about it, and all she's heard from her friends is that periods are the "worst." Ethan has friends who are good kids but they joke a lot about sex and occasionally look at pornographic images on their phones. He doesn't feel comfortable talking to his father about it, but he is very curious about the images and doesn't know what to do.

Jacob is curious about his own body. He sometimes finds a ball or toy to roll over his penis because it feels good and his penis changes size. However, his mom just swatted Jacob's hand when he touched himself during bath time and said, "Those are private parts. Don't touch!" These are pretty normal kids with lots of questions. If Mom and Dad can decide now to approach sexual development in an open, happy, healthy manner from this point forward, these three children can still move through their early sexual development with a healthier perspective and a greater closeness to their parents.

Talking about sexual anatomy and functioning may be scary for some parents. Most of us did not have parents who regularly and cheerfully discussed sexual development, so we might struggle a bit with being open about sexual development ourselves. As parents, we are in a privileged position because we can teach our children how their bodies are changing according to what we know from research and experience, and we are also blessed to teach our children about Heavenly Father's perspective on their sexuality (see table at the end of this chapter for general guidelines for discussions about sexuality as a function of child age). Elder Horacio A. Tenorio reminded us: "Parents have the inalienable right and the responsibility to educate their children. No inappropriate outsider should be allowed to dictate our family's values nor what our children are being taught. . . . A loving interview guided by the Spirit can give direction to our children's lives, bring about necessary adjustments or changes, and may even result in miracles."[1]

How Do Parents Initiate This Discussion?

The parents in our example decided now was the time to overcome their own fears and talk about sexual development openly after hearing at a devotional from their capable bishop that they should have been talking about sexuality with their children since they were very young and that this would have made conversations much easier. They learned that talking about sex and sexual development is usually best done as a couple and that there is never a time too late to start. We know that an element of sexual wholeness is that sex occurs within a relationship, so it is helpful for children to see both Mom and Dad talking about sex and reaffirming that sex is an important and happy part of their relationship. Listening to this advice, these parents found a time and place that was free of distractions and invited Katy to visit with them. Here is an example conversation with Katy, who is now fourteen.

They open the conversation by saying something like, "We haven't been as open and clear about sexual development as we know we should be. So we are trying to make some changes and talk about how our bodies develop, feel, and work during this time in your life and later in your life as well. This might be awkward for all of us at first, but we know Heavenly Father views our sexual nature as divine and wonderful. So we know that if we try to ask and answer questions without shame or fear, we all are going to be better off. Katy, we hope you will feel closer to us, and we know we will all feel more joy when we can discuss how marvelous our bodies are and how sexuality is part of our mortal development that helps us feel closer to God. While you might already know some of the things we talk about, it will be helpful for us to cover some of the very basics so we can all make sure we understand the same things and we can talk about them from a spiritual perspective."

The conversation continues by looking at Figure 1. The parents talk about how they have seen physical changes in Katy that have transformed her from a little girl to a beautiful young woman. She has breasts, her shape has changed somewhat, and she is now menstruating. The parents will counteract the many negative messages from media and peers about menstruation by explaining the miraculous monthly process that a woman's body goes through to be ready to conceive, nourish, and carry a baby. A woman's breasts will continue to nourish the baby after it is born. These parents are in a position to explain that the female body is literally a portal for spirits to pass through into mortality. How wonderful is that?

The parents might then refer to Figures 2 through 4 to explain that each month, a woman's ovaries release an egg that could be fertilized by her husband's sperm through sexual intercourse (when the penis penetrates the vagina—we'll talk a little more about this in a minute). For the egg to be fertilized it must make a long journey and travel from the ovaries through the fallopian tubes to the uterine cavity. This process is so precise that each month when the egg is not fertilized, the woman experiences a period, or a flow of blood, to help shed the lining of the uterus and prepare again for the next month. This is a complex process, and it happens each month! All to ensure that babies can grow in a safe and nurturing environment. Women are entrusted with providing this portal and protecting the embryo and fetus as it develops. A woman's womb protects and develops life, and her breasts nourish life. This is a beautiful stewardship. Women's bodies allow them to be cocreators with God.

Figure 3 might be particularly helpful in discussing another important aspect of each person's sexual nature. Both men and women feel sexual arousal. Sexual arousal can come from many sources, but certainly stimulating our body produces arousal. As women are aroused, their body begins to lubricate, which allows for easier penetration. Lubrication protects the delicate skin of the penis and tissue of the vaginal walls from serious irritation or harm. Figure 3 shows the female external sexual anatomy. Women, like men, may be aroused a number of ways. Women's breasts and genitals are high arousal areas that also have additional functions; however, the clitoris is specifically for sexual arousal. The clitoris is at the front of the labia majora above the urethral orifice.

The parents might continue by describing to Katy the sexual development of boys. It is important for our children to understand both male and female sexual functioning to have an appropriate perspective of sexuality. Figures 5 through 8 show the sexual organs of a man (Figures 7 and 8 show a circumcised and uncircumcised penis, respectively). Men's sexual organs are mainly on the outside of their bodies and are therefore a little easier to understand and explain. A man may feel arousal from being touched on many areas of the body, but the penis is the most sensitive to touch. As a man becomes aroused, blood flows to the penis and surrounding area, and this blood flow produces an erection—a firm penis. In order to penetrate the vagina, a penis needs to be firm, so this is not only a pleasurable process but a necessary one as well. For men, the urethra carries both urine and semen (which contains sperm). When a man has an erection, the flow of urine is blocked, and only semen is allowed through the penis by a process called ejaculation.

The scrotum is a loose pouch of skin that protects the testes. The scrotum keeps the testes at a temperature that is slightly lower than the rest of the body. This environment allows for the production of sperm and testosterone. Muscles in the scrotum allow the body to keep the testes closer to the body in colder temperatures and hang looser and away from the body

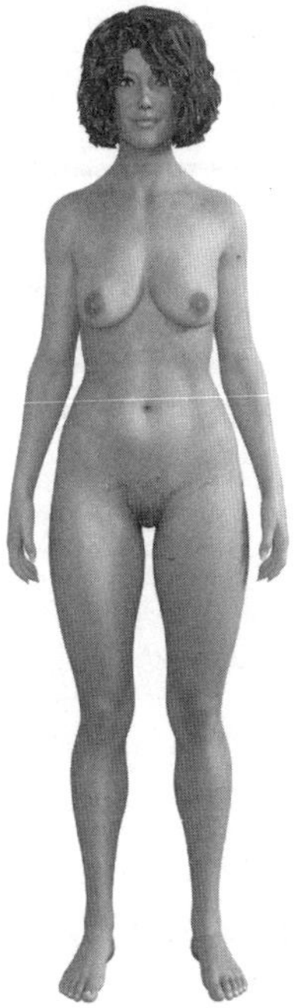

Figure 1.

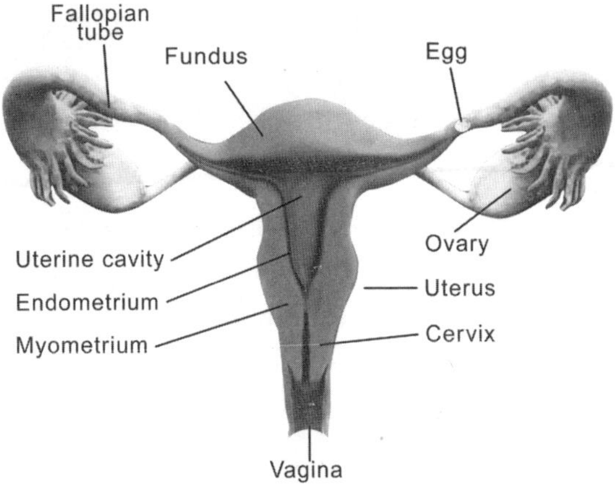

Figure 2.

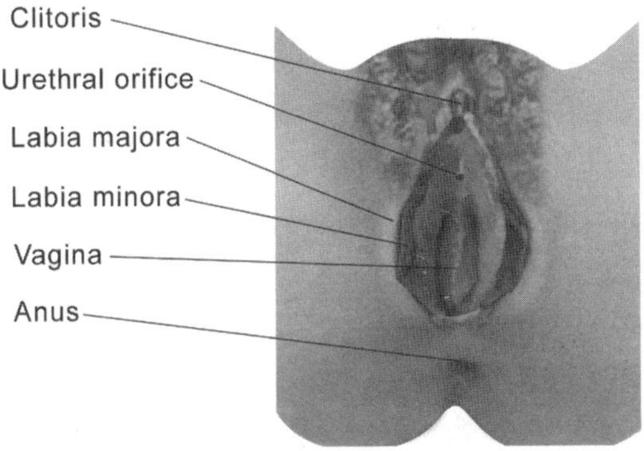

Figure 3.

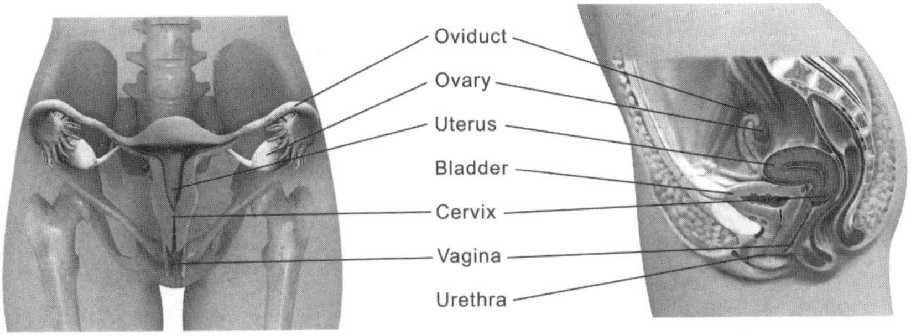

Figure 4.

in warmer temperatures. Our bodies are capable of functioning in an intricate and carefully designed way.

This discussion enables the parents to help Katy better understand Heavenly Father's plan, how her body is an important element of the plan, and how her mortal experience is enhanced by this elaborate sexual development process. Depending on Katy's responsiveness and inquisitiveness, this conversation may be extended or shortened so that it is not overwhelming.

Parents can use these same figures to talk with younger and older children about sexual development, as they feel is appropriate. These conversations will take place over many years and will each build on previous conversations. The goal is to create a regular dialogue that allows sex to be a normal topic that is comfortably discussed whenever there is an appropriate opportunity. The parents could use these same diagrams to show two-year-old Jacob how his body is working. When Jacob stimulates his penis, it fills with blood and becomes erect. They could also show Jacob how his anus is part of his digestive system and that as food moves through his body, the parts that are not used in the body are eliminated through the colon and anus. The parents could use the figures to help prepare their middle son, Ethan, for the changes he is experiencing or about to experience during maturation. This should include a discussion about how as he becomes sexually mature it will be common for him to experience nocturnal emissions (or wet dreams), which are usually associated with dreams of a sexual nature, that allow his body to dispel semen through ejaculation. These are not something to feel guilty about but are normal processes of maturation. Parents may also refer to Chapter 9 when talking to Ethan about masturbation. These figures can be used over

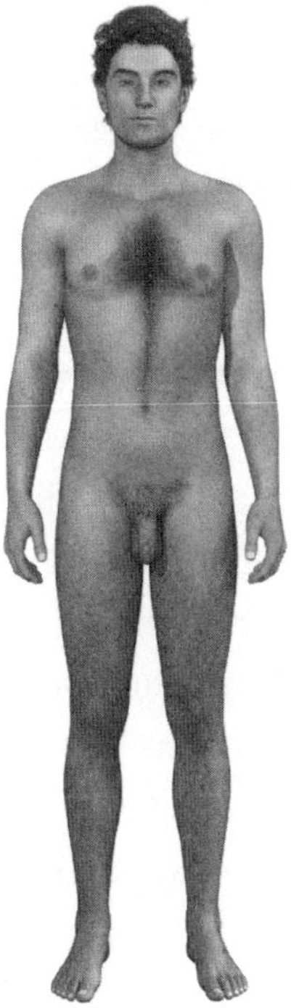

Figure 5.

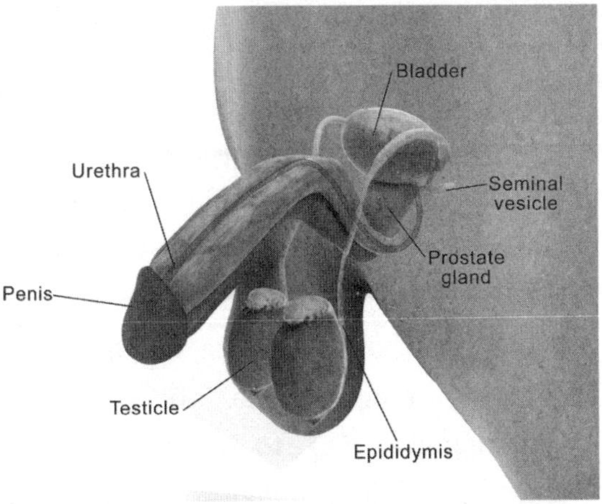

Figure 6.

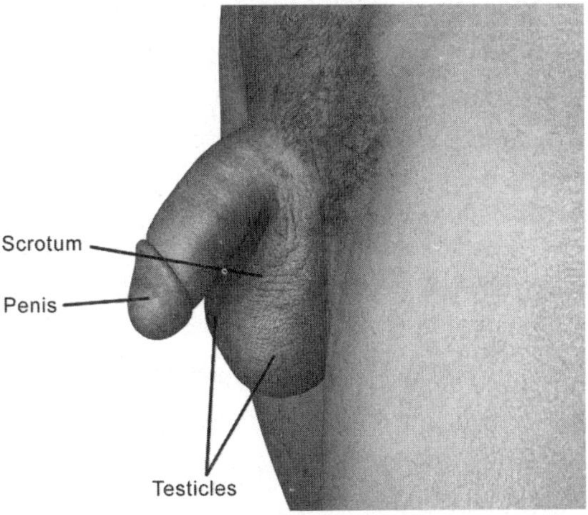

Figure 7.

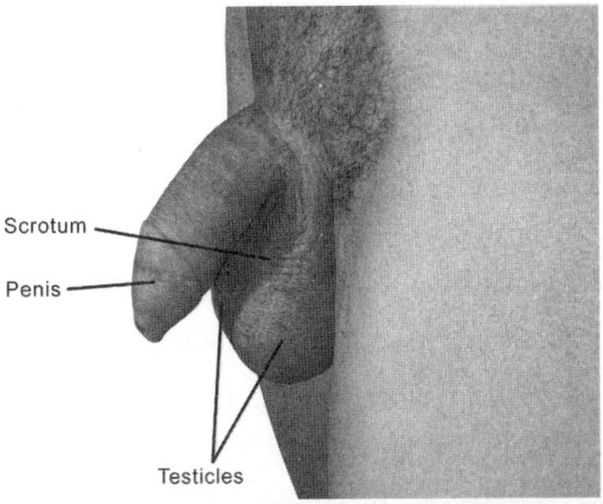

Figure 8.

and over throughout children's early years to better explain the sexual process and how their bodies work. While using these figures may feel uncomfortable to some parents, they provide a helpful tool for understanding our wonderful bodies and helping our children to understand their own development. It will be important to talk with all children about how what they focus their thoughts on can also lead to sexual arousal, and it is an important time to learn to have both chaste actions and chaste thoughts by thinking of all people as their brothers and sisters rather than as sexual objects. Of course, parents should carefully consider each individual child and what he or she might be ready for and when, but we would encourage you to step outside of your comfort zone and allow open conversation as much as possible.

Discussion by Celebrating Puberty

In addition to discussing physical, social, and emotional consequences of puberty, parents should also discuss with their children the spiritual consequences of puberty. In other words, what meaning do our children give to the changes they are experiencing? We believe that how parents approach and discuss puberty and the changes associated with it will in great part shape the meaning that children give to sexual development. In the United States and much of the Western world, physical and sexual changes in the body are considered to be issues of great privacy and sometimes even embarrassment. These are generally not things that we openly discuss and certainly are not things that we celebrate. However, if you think about it for a moment, puberty is an amazing biological process that is triggered in the body and prepares young men and women to bear children. In a spiritual sense, this is a process that is one of the first steps toward us being capable of cocreation with our Heavenly Parents, and is clearly a biological process that has divine roots and branches. Marriage, bringing spirit children to this earth, and establishing families are central to the Lord's plan, and an essential part of all of these events is reaching puberty. Is this not something to celebrate rather than be embarrassed about? Could celebrating puberty help children focus more on the spiritual aspects of puberty and sexuality and less on the physical and emotional?

In some cultures and religions, manhood and womanhood, or coming of age, are celebrated. Young Jewish girls and boys go through Bat or Bar Mitzvah at age twelve or thirteen as a means of welcoming the child into the world of adulthood and starting him or her on the path of both the responsibilities and opportunities that come along with being a Jewish man or woman. Many Latin American cultures celebrate a young woman's *quinceañera*, or her fifteenth birthday party, as a special time when female children make the transition to womanhood. While your family may not resonate with these particular puberty celebrations, the motivation behind these behaviors is to celebrate the transition from being a child to being a woman or a man—to celebrate the power of procreation, to celebrate virtue. The celebration of such events helps us to understand and appreciate gender more fully and to acknowledge our divine roles as men and women. And though the physical changes that go along with the transition to manhood and womanhood don't have to be a part of these celebrations, they can be given meaning by being placed in this framework. If we treat monthly menstrual periods as a private annoyance at best and a painful burden at worst, and wet dreams as secretive and even dirty or sinful, children will have a very different feeling about how their new biological abilities relate to their spiritual roles than if these changes are placed in a more positive light and within a more eternal perspective. We certainly acknowledge that menstrual periods can be painful and frustrating and that erections and unintended ejaculation can be embarrassing. But if we can help our children to understand the purpose behind these bodily functions and focus on their spiritual development, puberty will be a much more positive experience and will contribute to healthy sexuality.

So what do we already do as Latter-day Saints to celebrate growth to adulthood and help our children to understand their divine nature and sexuality? Certainly the Young Men and Young Women programs of the Church address these developmental tasks by celebrating advancement from deacon to teacher to priest and from Beehive to Mia Maid to Laurel. These are public acts in which youth are brought to the front of the chapel and celebrated for their worthiness and are publicly advanced to the next "level." These are important rites of passage and help youth to learn about their roles and responsibilities in the Church and as men and women. While laudable, however, these traditions have little to do with puberty and physical development, so teens might not make the connection between these advancements and the interplay between their divine physical and spiritual development as sons and daughters of God.

While we would strongly discourage parents from announcing their daughter's first menstruation over the pulpit (especially if they would like her to speak to them at some point during the next five years), we do think it's worth pondering how families could celebrate puberty within their own homes in a way that would potentially change how children think about physical development and that would contribute to healthy sexuality and spirituality.

When we discuss these topics in class, most of our students admit that their parents did nothing when they reached puberty or that they were slipped a box of tampons and a note with an offhand offer for follow-up conversations if needed. As mentioned earlier, males note almost no discussions with their parents prior to puberty, and maybe something as informal as a pat on the back from Dad and a grimace from Mom when they inquire about their first wet dream (if they even discuss it with parents at all). However, other students have mentioned that their dad took each of his girls out to dinner when they had their first period to celebrate womanhood, or that the dad and all the older sons went out for ice cream when the youngest son turned sixteen and talked about being a man and a father. One student even reported having her father make her whole family uterus-shaped pancakes in celebration of her menstruation, which she had clearly not yet completely forgiven him for. Although this last example may seem a little bit over the top, the father's heart was in the right place, and this family was promoting open communication about natural physical changes that should be sacred, but not secret, and that should be celebrated. Most ideas we hear about puberty rituals are nothing big or showy, but they have left an impact on these students as they have reflected on what it means to come of age sexually.

Whether it's a big gesture or a small one, establishing family rituals surrounding puberty, or a child's coming of age, is worth considering and discussing with your spouse. Barbara Fiese, professor of human development and family studies at the University of Illinois, suggests that family rituals have a central place in our lives, tying children to their past, increasing family cohesion, and encouraging self-reflection and personal improvement for the future. Family rituals provide meaning and memories for children and parents alike and provide a stability and consistency for children that is important for development. Think of your family. What rituals do you have? Do you do something every year for your daughter's birthday? Are there things you do with your son after every priesthood session of general conference? Do you have songs you sing or scriptures you read every Christmas? Even daily family prayer and weekly family home evening are considered family rituals, and while children may not remember exactly what was taught or all activities and treats that were lovingly planned, they will remember the tradition. Elder David A. Bednar reminded us, speaking about spiritual family rituals, "They likely would not identify a particular prayer or a specific instance of scripture study or an especially meaningful family home evening lesson as the defining moment in their spiritual development. What they would say they remember is that as a family we were consistent."[2] What we are suggesting is that if we treat puberty as merely an inconvenient physical change that has some undesired emotional consequences, that is how our children will come to feel about their experience and these functions of their body. However, if we treat puberty as the physical manifestation of a divine and eternal aspect of our spiritual progression, and perhaps do this through the use of a celebration of manhood or womanhood, our children will know what to expect, will feel positively about their puberty experience, and will integrate their experience and development with their sexual and spiritual progression. We recommend you start by talking with your children about puberty and what to expect. And if it doesn't feel too radical for you, consider thinking of a way you might be able to make this transition special for your children as they begin to think about being a mother or father.

BIRTH–3 YEARS OLD

Sexual Development

Vocabulary. Vocabulary. Vocabulary. Vocabulary is an important element for healthy sexual development. Name body parts correctly. Use vocabulary like penis, vagina, breasts, nipple, etc. These words will be common and comfortable if they are used from the start. This is a time to gain confidence in our use of proper vocabulary.

Emotional Development

Explain how amazing bodies are. Have your child look at how the body heals, moves, and grows. Explain, you are valuable not only because of your amazing body but because of your beautiful mind and spirit. You are valuable because you are a daughter or son of God.

Physical Development

Point out to your children how they are getting bigger, stronger, and more skilled. Help them understand that these changes prepare them for other physical and emotional changes later. Change can be frustrating, but it is helpful for children to see that it is a process and soon they will master whatever challenges them.

3–7 YEARS OLD

Sexual Development

Answer questions simply. No need to overwhelm children with information. Just answer questions in a simple way. Be available and happy to talk about thoughts or concerns—sexual or otherwise. Explain that our body is our own. We keep genitals private because this establishes healthy boundaries. We don't talk casually with others about genitals or sex.

Emotional Development

Remind your children that their thoughts and feelings are important to you. When they are sad, happy, or confused, you want to help them and comfort them. If children struggle to understand, identify, or express emotions, now is a good time to be their coach so they can better identify feelings and positively work through them. This will help your children better regulate emotions and behaviors later in development.

Physical Development

Most children do not experience strong sexual feelings at this point, but they are trying to understand how their bodies work. So curiosity is natural and motivates questions and exploration. Parents encourage positive feelings about bodies and bodily functions by explaining we respect and care for our bodies.

7–9 YEARS OLD

Sexual Development

Be straightforward. This is a time to give children accurate, complete information that will protect them from others' misrepresentations of sex and sexual relationships. Explain not only the mechanics of sexual intercourse but also the idea that healthy sex occurs within marriage because that is where these feelings and expressions are most likely to be protected and kept sacred. Give the message that sex is wondrous and an important part of who we are.

Emotional Development

Express confidence in how your children think through difficult topics or emotions. Explain that their hard work prepares them to solve problems and handle challenges. We live in a hypersexualized environment, and this can create negative sexual attitudes and behaviors. Help them understand sexual expression is beautiful and meant to strengthen a marriage. Encourage conversations about emotions. This will establish stronger connections for times when sexual feelings are new and arousal needs to be better understood.

Physical Development

Prepare your children for the physical changes that are coming over the next few years. Occasionally, review how bodies change and prepare for sexual maturity. Be clear about anatomy. Review diagrams of male and female bodies. Answer questions regularly and emphasize your feelings of confidence in their ability to be successful in this amazing physical change.

9–12 YEARS OLD

Sexual Development

Encourage greater understanding. Gaining a sense of mastery with our body is not always easy. Just as it is hard to master soccer or the piano, understanding our sexual development, feelings, and arousal takes time. Reassure children that you are the best source of information and can help them understand this process. Although this process is complex, it is wonderful and a joyful part of our nature. Talk about how boys and girls are different in some ways and the same in some ways.

Emotional Development

Children are becoming more emotionally independent but will likely remain emotionally close to their parents if parents value the children's ideas and thoughts. Be careful to be a coach, not a lecturer. Discussions are the goal. Your child's body is preparing to be fully mature—physically and sexually. However, emotional maturity takes much longer and requires patience and practice. Children may feel sexual attraction to others during this time period. Talk about this and how expanding socially is an important part of their sexual development.

Physical Development

Noticeable physical changes occur for both boys and girls during this time period. Talking about it helps children feel more comfortable and confident during this adjustment. Be aware of signs of negative body image and address these. Prepare your children for future changes by regularly talking about the entire process. Children have renewed interest in the physical process when they are experiencing some of these changes.

TEENAGERS

Sexual Development

Gaining mastery. Understanding and mastering sexual feelings is complicated and will likely require practice. Teenagers need encouragement to maintain sexual standards and regular in-depth conversations about their own thoughts, feelings, and behaviors. Weekly conversations give children an opportunity to ask questions, voice concerns, and feel support. Discussion can include questions about arousal: If you are aroused, do you need to act on the arousal or can it be controlled? What prompts arousal? Do both boys and girls feel arousal? What are physical signs of arousal?

Emotional Development

Remember that intimacy is the goal in our relationships with our children AND the goal of their future sexual relationships. Learning to talk about emotions is a fundamental aspect of sexual development. Teens can make progress in identifying, expressing, and understanding their emotions and arousal through comfortable conversations. Ideas to open conversations could include these questions or topics: Why is it best to not talk casually with others about sex? What are some common myths about sex? How can sex be misused? How can we show affection for others? What would you do or say to avoid or get out of an interaction that was too sexual? Why is emotional intimacy important?

Physical Development

Many physical changes are still occurring. Talking openly about these changes helps teens to ask questions and normalize their experience. Explain that physical maturity does not always mean emotional maturity. Although our bodies are sexually mature, emotionally we are still maturing. We are not yet ready to make commitments needed for sexual wholeness. Reserving our sexual expression for marriage gives us time to emotionally develop and maintain safe and appropriate boundaries.

Chapter Highlights

Helping children have the language to describe their bodies will help them be more aware of what they might be feeling sexually. Part of open communication is for both parents and children to be comfortable talking openly about our wonderful bodies and all they are and can do, in developmentally appropriate ways.

While puberty and sexuality are sacred, they need not be secret. Consider finding ways that you and your child might celebrate the transition to adulthood and all that this means physically, emotionally, sexually, spiritually, and eternally.

Create opportunities for regular discussions about sex. Ask your children how they are doing, what they are experiencing, what their peers talk about, and how they feel about their bodies and arousal.

Thought Questions

Are you comfortable talking about the details of maturation? Is your child comfortable talking about the details of maturation? If not, how could you encourage more comfortable, regular conversations?

Do you use the correct terms for body parts and their functions?

What changes can you make in how you think about puberty so that you can teach your children to think about these physical changes as part of their spiritual progression?

Do you like the idea of a puberty celebration (or a celebration of manhood or womanhood), and if so, what are some ideas that you could try in your family?

Putting It into Practice

Use a family home evening and have a test on the human

body. Have diagrams of both a male and a female and see how many parts of the body the family can properly name. If that is easy, you could also talk about the function of each part. The activity can include a discussion on the wonderful gift of a mortal body and how Heavenly Father celebrates with us the proper use of our sexual nature.

When you talk with your children about puberty or development or their ability to create children, discuss it in a celebratory way and talk with them about all of the wonderful benefits of puberty before you complain about the hassles.

Plan a celebration (that fits your child's temperament) for when each reaches milestones of puberty. This could be a private celebration between you and your child or could be something that involves the whole family. It doesn't need to be linked to puberty but could celebrate any age you choose. Use these opportunities to celebrate manhood or womanhood with your child. Some ideas include taking your child out to a special meal, having a small family party, or getting your child a special gift that will help him or her prepare for parenthood.

Tell your children stories about your own puberty experience and how it was celebrated or how you wish perhaps it had been celebrated more. Ask your children for input about how your family can celebrate with them so that they have something to look forward to and look back upon as a meaningful experience.

Chapter 7

Body Image

Divine nature has nothing to do with external appearance.

Christina's daughter Savannah was always a relatively average girl in terms of weight—not overly heavy and not thin. But when she hit puberty, her metabolism slowed and she gained ten pounds. Savannah's brothers have been teasing her about her weight gain and have started calling her names. Christina also overheard Savannah and her father in the kitchen the other day when he casually commented that she might want to start watching what she eats. Christina has noticed that Savannah frequently comments that she is heavier than several of her friends who have not yet reached puberty, and her self-esteem is beginning to suffer. She spends long hours staring at herself in the mirror, pinching the skin on her arms and stomach, and when she sits downs she complains about how big her thighs look. Christina doesn't know what to say because she is an avid exerciser, goes to the gym six days a week, and eats a very low-fat diet. Christina also notices that despite her thinness, she is constantly putting down her own body, so she wonders how this must make Savannah feel. One day in Relief Society there was a lesson about beauty and what it means to be attractive on the inside. The teacher shared the importance of being healthy but assured the women that who they are on the inside is much more important than how they look on the outside. This lesson helped Christina to see how her own behavior might have been damaging her daughter's self-esteem and motivated her to be someone her daughter could talk to about her concerns. She realized that how her daughter felt about her body was influencing all other aspects of her life, including how she felt about her own self-worth.

The physical changes of puberty are often accompanied by body image issues, as a teenager's basal metabolic rate (or the minimal amount of energy that is used when resting) generally decreases about 15% and the ratio of fat to muscle increases markedly. These changes are often linked to decreases in self-esteem, especially for girls, which can have serious implications for how an understanding of sexuality develops. Though females are more prone to distorted body image than are males, and there is much more research on female body image than male body image, it is becoming increasingly common for young men to also obsess about weight and muscles, strength and leanness, and to place undue focus on how strong they are or how they don't stack up to the latest super-human movie icon. As parents and adults in the lives of young people, we can play a very important role in shaping how our children think about their bodies. Diane Jones, professor at the University of Washington, has found that parents shape their children's body image through their own attitudes and behaviors (including exercise and dieting behaviors) and through the comments they make about their own and their spouse's body shape. These parental attitudes and behaviors can lead to body dissatisfaction in children as young as five years old. In addition, we live in a society with mass media that bombards youth with unrealistic images of the ideal, so it is especially important that our children receive a different message from those close to them. It is a somewhat fine line to walk between promoting a healthy lifestyle and avoiding unhealthy attitudes and behaviors about eating. That being said, children and youth have a much better chance of developing a healthy self-image and understanding of the beauty of their bodies and their current and future sexuality if the adults in their lives model this behavior and teach correct principles.

From the time children are in nursery, they are encouraged to be fascinated with the wonder that is their bodies. Many of us are familiar with the Primary lesson that points out different body parts and celebrates all that they can do: the amazing colors we can see with our eyes on an afternoon in autumn, the variety of tastes we enjoy with our tongues when eating fruits that are sour and sweet, the joy of music and assorted sounds we hear with our ears when playing musical instruments, the numerous textures on our skin that send different sensations throughout our entire bodies. These processes are truly amazing. If you have ever watched an infant or young child enjoy his or her own body, there is much we can learn from this unabashed pride in an amazing gift that allows freedom and agency and joy in ever-increasing ways. Why is it, then, that the celebration of all that our bodies can do virtually disappears after the nursery-aged child moves to Primary? Instead, we begin to worry about whether or not our children will ever lose the baby fat that we so enjoyed when they were younger or whether they will start to develop unhealthy sexual behaviors. When someone isn't happy with how his or her body looks, researchers call it "body dissatisfaction," and most of us have some level of dissatisfaction. Charlotte Markey, professor at Rutgers University, in her book *Smart People Don't Diet*, said that 90% of women (and about 70% of teenage girls) and 75% of men experience body dissatisfaction, so it is something with which most of us are familiar. And it's not overly concerning if your child occasionally feels dissatisfied with one or two things about his or her body. But if your child is obsessing about how he or she looks or his or her weight or how the opposite sex thinks about his or her body—this is something parents need to take notice of and try to address before the impact is long-lasting (you can take the survey at the end of this chapter to see how high your or your child's body dissatisfaction is).

A healthy and satisfying sexual relationship is built on appreciation, love, and understanding of our bodies. People who are ashamed of their bodies have a very difficult time freely enjoying the intimacy, nudity, and vulnerability that are a part of healthy sexual expression. Research on body image and sexuality suggests that adults with body dissatisfaction have lower quality sexual relationships, in part because they are worried about how their naked bodies look (more common for women) and how they function (more common for men). In his research on body image and sexual functioning, Michael Wiederman, professor of psychology at Columbia College, has consistently found that men and women who report more self-consciousness about their bodies also report less pleasure and enjoyment during sexual activity because they are more focused on their own bodies than on their partner and the intimate experience.

Because an individual's feelings about his or her own body are formed in large part during childhood and the teen years, there is much we can do to help our children in this regard. How can we provide a healthy environment for our children while also encouraging body satisfaction? Dr. Melissa Smith, licensed psychologist and certified eating disorder specialist, suggests a number of strategies based on research in this area, and we hope that at least one or two of them will resonate with your own family and can be relatively easily implemented.

Strategy #1: Establish Healthy Lifestyle Patterns as a Family

Beyond the somewhat obvious suggestions of increasing the amount of whole foods, fruits and vegetables, and home-cooked meals while limiting overly processed foods, families can work at being healthy together and can establish patterns of physical activity that can become a way of life and help children to appreciate all the wonderful things their bodies can do. We can play *with* our children, creating family time around physical activity and making it something to look forward to rather than something that must be done. We can make sports and activities part of our weekly family home evening and allow our children to choose the physical activities they might enjoy—for example, going on a family bike ride, a walk to the park, or registering for a 5K run as a family. We can then point out all the wonderful things our bodies can do and how important keeping them healthy can be. As part of these efforts, adults should be cautious not to do anything that would negatively impact body image and should not allow siblings or others to make negative comments. For example, we should avoid negative comments about our own bodies or our children's bodies, and we should not allow family members to tease one another about body shapes, sizes, or abilities. When parents participate with their children in physical activities and help them understand how the foods they eat influence their moods and energy levels in appropriate ways, all with the purpose of helping them to experience the joys of life more fully rather than look a certain way, they can significantly help children develop a lifelong interest and enjoyment of good foods and active lifestyles.

Strategy #2: Help Children Be Critical Consumers of Media

One of the most important things parents can do to help their teens to be emotionally, physically, spiritually, and sexually healthy is to encourage them to be critical consumers of media. We need to educate our children about the way that advertising works and how impractical pictures seen on television and in magazines are, because there is a clear link between teens' body dissatisfaction and their exposure to commercials and magazines that portray idealized female thinness or male muscularity. Nearly all media images are reconstructions; they are not reflections of reality. Nearly every magazine cover and billboard our children pass has been airbrushed, photoshopped, and in many cases, altered significantly with advanced technology. It is important for teens (and parents!) to realize that these images are not real. We can also point out to teens manipulative advertising that encourages unhealthy thinness and is often misleading and entirely ineffective, such as diet pills that claim to help one lose weight without exercising, or ads that focus entirely on the ideal of the external body, often portraying the female body in sexual and suggestive ways. There are other, more subtle forms of harmful advertising that we can help teens recognize, like certain promotions of foods that suggest you'll become fat if you eat anything other than their product. In contrast, we can point out good advertising that promotes beauty in all shapes and sizes and highlights healthy body function (e.g., having strong legs so you can bounce your grandchildren on them). Elder Jeffrey R. Holland said, "At some point the problem becomes what the Book of Mormon called 'vain imaginations,' and in secular society both vanity and imagination run wild. One would truly need a great and spacious makeup kit to compete with beauty as portrayed in media all around us."[1] Thus, one key thing we can do to help our children develop healthy body image and healthy sexuality is to help them to recognize what is real and what is merely part of our imagination, fed by the media.

Strategy #3: Help Children Love Their Own Bodies

Many teens assume that being ideally thin or muscular and athletic is associated with being happy, and that if they were only thinner or stronger they would be more popular, get more dates, and be more attractive to the opposite sex. It is important for us to help both our girls and our boys to look beyond physical appearance and to realize that true happiness and emotional and sexual connection come from establishing enduring positive character traits and relationships. For parents, the first step in helping our children with this is to recognize our own biases regarding external appearance. Do you joke or make negative references about your own weight, baldness, height, or another aspect of your external appearance? Do you verbally admire others for having lost weight or make negative comments when someone has gained weight? Children have an excellent memory for comments that are made in this regard, especially if they're made directly about the child (e.g., "It looks like you've gained some weight!"). But even if comments are made about others, inferences are made by our children. So if Mom consistently comments on how amazing the latest actor's muscles are or if Dad makes frequent mention of how much weight the neighbors have gained, children are likely to wonder what their parents think of *their* external appearance and what that means for their worth.

Once we have recognized our own biases, we can start helping our children love their bodies by improving our behavior and encouraging healthy body image. Elder Holland said, "If adults are preoccupied with appearance—tucking and nipping and implanting and remodeling everything that can be remodeled—those pressures and anxieties will certainly seep through to children."[2] Rather, we can help children celebrate and appreciate their natural and healthy body shape and understand that external appearance says very little about who individuals are and how much value they have. If your son comments on how stunning some girl at school is, you could acknowledge that and then ask him what her other positive traits are or whether or not she treats others well. When your daughter begins to focus on her developing body and comments that other girls are using their bodies to get sexual attention, you could try to encourage her to focus on her accomplishments and hard work rather than external appearance and to think of her body as a highly effective tool or instrument (or gift!) rather than an ornament. Another suggestion is to help children appreciate their bodies by focusing on the positives such as how well their bodies work or what a blessing it is to have a body. Watch babies enjoy their bodies and help teens understand the beauty of their bodies and all their functions, including the sexual. These steps may be difficult for some who are deeply entrenched in their own biases about weight and external appearance and have potentially developed some bad habits of thinking and behaving in ways that might discourage healthy body image, but it is never too late to start. Just make one change at a time.

Strategy #4: Help Children Develop Their Spirituality

Our bodies are a gift from our Heavenly Father, and as such, it should be one of our highest priorities to take care of them as we would any other precious gift. As few of us would ever receive a gift and then promptly and repeatedly tell the giver how unhappy we are with said gift, parents can help their children to understand the importance of being grateful for their bodies and not allowing realistic variations in healthy body size or shape to impact self-worth and sexuality. How our children perceive their bodies spiritually is also closely tied to sexuality. Susan W. Tanner said, "What would happen if we truly treated our bodies as temples? The result would be a dramatic increase in chastity, modesty, observance of the Word of Wisdom, and a similar decrease in the problems of pornography and abuse, for we would regard the body, like the temple, as a sacred sanctuary of the Spirit. Just as no unclean thing may enter the temple, we would be vigilant to keep impurity of any sort from entering the temple of our bodies."[3] Believing that one is a child of God and of infinite worth is simply not compatible with transgressions involving the body and with the idea that one's worth is dependent on external appearance.

Accepting one's worth regardless of external appearance can be especially difficult for physically attractive young men and women who can more easily fall back on their looks, to the detriment of their character. This is exacerbated when parents and leaders continually and solely praise youth for their beauty or their stature and strength. President Russell M. Nelson said, "Your Heavenly Father has known you for a very long time. You, as His son or daughter, were chosen by Him to come to earth at this precise time, to be a leader in His great work on earth. You were chosen not for your bodily characteristics but for your spiritual attributes, such as bravery, courage, integrity of heart, a thirst for truth, a hunger for wisdom, and a desire to serve others."[4] We can help young people develop a deep and abiding testimony of their own individual worth in the sight of God and spend more time developing enduring attributes that will be with them in the eternities. This can be accomplished by helping youth truly understand their individual purpose, strengths, and gifts and focus on improving on areas of weakness. As President Boyd K. Packer said, "Your body really is the instrument of your mind and the foundation of your character."[5] Optimal physical health is central to optimal spiritual health, and helping teens to understand this can go a long way to preventing body image problems and helping children understand their worth.

In short, if teens believe their worth is tied up in their physical appearance, this impacts future relationships and their understanding of sexuality. Sexuality is not purely based on physical attraction (especially not as the world defines physical attraction) but is about emotional and spiritual connection as well—and the combination of these can lead to sexual wholeness. Like Christina and Savannah in the example at the beginning of this chapter, parents and siblings play an important role in the development of one's body image and can help set a foundation of confidence and love of self from a very early age, if we are careful and aware of our own biases and how they might impact young children and teenagers.

Chapter Highlights

How parents feel about their own bodies will influence how they parent and how children feel about their bodies.

Helping children have positive body image is central to healthy sexuality, so remember to promote health and an active lifestyle with your family, teach your children to be critical consumers of media, help your children to love their own bodies and all the capabilities they have, and help your children improve their spirituality. These four steps will aid children in developing healthy body image and self-esteem.

Thought Questions

When was the last time you personally felt full of gratitude for your wonderful body? When was the last time you offered a prayer full of gratitude to God for the body you enjoy?

How has the way that you view your body impacted your sexuality?

Is there anything you're doing in your interactions with your children that might be contributing to their body image or body dissatisfaction?

Putting It into Practice

If you hike, run, bike, walk, swim, or do another physical activity as a family and then note your soreness or enjoy the "runner's high" together, you can exult in your bodies' capacities and encourage each other to set good physical health goals and then celebrate achieving them. This can and should be done without any reference to reaching an unrealistic body type, pressuring a child to lose weight, etc. Rather, the goal is to learn to be physically active and healthy to better show appreciation for your body and enjoy it more.

Talk openly with your spouse and your children about the biases they may already hold about physical appearance, and challenge each other to avoid a focus on external appearance and instead to focus on how to live a healthy lifestyle and appreciate your body.

Ask your children to share insecurities about their own bodies and suggest ways they can reframe their thoughts. Have them do the same for you.

When you see a magazine cover or an advertisement, remind your children that the images they see are photoshopped and do not reflect reality.

Answer the questions below (for yourself and your child) to see how high your body dissatisfaction or obsession with weight loss is. If you answer YES to more than two of these questions, what are you doing that might be influencing your child's body image? If your child answers YES to more than two of these questions, what ideas from this chapter can you implement to help your child focus on a healthy lifestyle instead of focusing on body image?

Body Image Questions

Do you worry more than most people your age about your body or weight?

Are you afraid of gaining weight?

Have you ever gone on a diet?

Are your weight and body image very important to you compared to other things in your life?

Do you often feel fat?

Chapter 8

Modesty and Sexuality

Modesty is more than the length of a skirt.

Isabella has been trying to help her daughter and son understand the importance of modesty. She was ten when she first heard a lesson on dressing modestly, and in subsequent years she repeatedly heard lessons about dress length and not wearing revealing or tight clothes. She overheard her son telling her daughter that one reason for modesty is that it was important to help young men keep their thoughts pure. He said that if young women wore something that was revealing, they might be causing a boy to have sexual thoughts. Isabella's daughter told her that she could see the need to dress modestly, but the lessons sometimes caused her to feel shameful about her body and to feel anxiety about how boys looked at her. They even fought sometimes because her daughter started to focus much more on how she dressed and really didn't understand why she needed to be modest. Eventually her daughter started to push the boundaries and wear shorter skirts and more revealing tops because she couldn't justify why she shouldn't wear clothes that accentuated her figure. Finally, Isabella sat down with her daughter and her son and asked them why they thought modesty was important and how it applied to both of them. They had a serious conversation about the reasons to value modesty and how modesty is connected to developing healthy sexuality. This helped Isabella's children to feel much better and to understand the reasons behind the doctrine, which in turn increased their desire to dress and act modestly.

Modesty is a tricky topic for many people in the Church. Sometimes it is a topic only taught to girls and it only focuses on dress. However, many parents have questioned that approach because we know that modesty is much more than the length of a dress or the way clothes fit. We also know that our boys need to be taught the importance of modesty as well. Modesty is not just about covering our bodies. Modesty really encompasses how we feel, think, and behave. So how can we as parents teach this deeper meaning of modesty to our young men and women?

It may help to understand the definitions of modesty: lack of pretentiousness (which is attempting to impress people with greater importance than we possess), a regard for decency, simplicity, and the act of showing reserve. When we describe a modest home, we are not describing whether the windows are "covered up" and whether the decorations are "revealing." Instead we are describing an attitude of reserve and a lack of pretentiousness. The same attitude applies to personal modesty. Teaching our children to think, feel, and behave modestly requires that we have discussions of modest living as well as modest dress. Sister Carol F. McConkie reminded us: "Modesty is not vain or boastful. Modest people do not use their bodies or their behavior to seek approval from the world or to draw attention to their own real or supposed accomplishments or desirable attributes."[1]

Today's culture barrages adults and children alike with anti-modesty messages. Modesty is not encouraged by society. In fact, our culture discourages modest thought, behavior, and dress. Self-effacement, humility, and unpretentiousness are not the traits taught in music videos, the business world, or at sporting events. At times, modesty may be mocked as an inability to be bold, stand out, or love ourselves. But modesty doesn't mean being a goody-two-shoes or a doormat. When we teach that modesty includes our thoughts and behaviors as well as our dress, our children are better prepared to combat the never-ending emphasis on physical beauty, sexy appearance, and physical evaluations (for more, see Chapter 7 on body image). As we remember that the Savior encouraged us to acknowledge our dependence on Him, it may be easier to maintain a feeling of modesty.

Sexual Modesty Is an Antidote to Many Negative Messages around Us

Let's use a new term here to describe the opposite of our current culture: *sexual modesty.* Sexual modesty is based on the idea that the part of ourselves that is sexual, including how we look, act, and feel that draws attention to our sexuality and stimulates sexual thoughts in ourselves and others, is only reserved for our spouse or future spouse. Parents can teach children that when we hold this part of ourselves sacred it strengthens our understanding of our divinity and increases holiness. In this way, modesty and sexuality combine to have greater power to bond and hold together future marriage, because it is reserved for marriage. Our modesty and sexuality are intricately intertwined because one, modesty, sets the boundaries around the other, sexuality. In this way, sexuality becomes synonymous with only one relationship, one other person, one covenant. Modesty then is like the invisible force field that surrounds our sexuality, keeping inside what belongs inside and rejecting everything else, which should stay outside. Sexual modesty is the exact opposite of exhibitionism or voyeurism.

Our world is saturated with exhibitionist images, text, and programs that stimulate the voyeuristic parts of people. Exhibitionism occurs when we expose sacred and private parts of ourselves such as our bodies, our sexual experiences, or our lives for the purpose of gaining attention. Voyeurism is viewing exhibitionistic portrayals as a form of entertainment. Our baser selves can be attracted to private, sensitive, sexual material that others are willing to portray in the media or in our social circles. This is why some of the most popular shows are "reality" shows that are based on people who are willing to be exhibitionists by drawing in viewers who are voyeuristic. Even less sexualized media forms, such as Facebook or Instagram, may encourage us to focus on ourselves and compare our appearance, accomplishments, and relationships to others. We begin to focus on the smallest details in our lives and lose sight of more important changes we need to address, like forgiveness or gentleness. Social media makes it all too easy to chat or post something that boasts about successes or reveals parts of our lives or our bodies that should remain private. Both young men and young women may need some counsel and guidance about what is modest behavior on social media outlets. As our culture changes and we are surrounded by these types of behaviors and practices, it is difficult to remember that central to the healthy practice of sexuality, and even relationship development, is the concept of privacy. We are not private because we are prudes or insecure.

We are private because certain aspects of ourselves are only shared with our spouses, and the more we honor these boundaries around our current or future marriages, the more these relationships can stay exclusive. This is absolutely necessary for the building of trust. This is the essence of sexual modesty.

Sexual modesty teaches that sexual images or thoughts of someone outside of the marriage should not be allowed to penetrate the marriage. When we understand modesty in this way, we can see the need to emphasize modesty to both our young men and young women. As parents teach their children about sexual modesty, other messages easily follow: a modest person would not provocatively dress, speak, or act in any way that drew attention to their sexuality and body except within the private space of marriage.

Modesty Is Not about Controlling Others' Behavior

Young women are not responsible for the thoughts of young men. This is an important point, as some people unintentionally or carelessly imply that if young women are immodest in dress, they hold some blame for young men's sexual thoughts. However, we are each responsible for our own thoughts and actions. Young women also feel sexual attraction, and when boys draw attention to their bodies by the way they dress or act, young women are equally capable of struggling with heightened arousal. Our children can find strength in having those with similar values around them, but we must never fall into the trap of blaming others. Cultivating the Spirit is the antidote to impure thought. We can teach our young men and women to be more mindful about how they dress and behave. We can visit with our children about how their dress and behavior may impact their ability to feel the Spirit. Modest thought and behavior are important guards of our spiritual, physical, and emotional security. Modesty adds a protective layer between us and the enemy of our soul. We need to teach our young men and women that they alone determine their thoughts. If young men have inappropriate thoughts because of how a girl is dressed, like Joseph of Egypt who "fled, and got him out" (Genesis 39:12), they alone are responsible for their thoughts and behaviors. Joseph developed into a strong spiritual man by taking personal responsibility for his thoughts and behaviors.

When blame is transferred to young women for the inappropriate thoughts or behaviors of young men, we undermine the principles of personal responsibility and agency. Of course, we have seen both young men and young women encourage inappropriate thoughts and behavior. We know that negative influences are out there. But transferring blame does not strengthen our children. As parents we can help our children by frankly addressing modesty. If girls are dressed provocatively, parents can talk with their boys about how to avoid being around that kind of temptation without making others feel judged or shameful. No doubt, both boys and girls are responsible for their own thoughts, but youth who embrace modesty will lift all those around them.

Living a Modest Life

Finally, modest thought not only means refraining from using our bodies to gain attention but also from using our words, behaviors, money, or anything in our control to draw extra attention to ourselves. When we live modestly, we're less likely to live above our means, wear clothes (whether they cover us or not) that draw excessive attention to our body, or use our education or talent to diminish others. Alma reminded the Nephites of modest living as he asked them, "Will ye still persist in the wearing of costly apparel and setting your hearts upon the vain things of the world, upon your riches?" (Alma 5:53). Our intellect, our body, and our talents are given to us to glorify God. Ammon was described as "being wise, yet harmless" (Alma 18:22). Parents who teach this broader meaning of modesty can, like Ammon, emphasize that we can use our skill and abilities for good—not to gloat in our advantage or to use our intellect to make others feel small, but to teach and build. Sister Linda K. Burton, former Relief Society General President, commented, "Brothers and sisters, we need each other! As covenant-keeping women and men, we need to lift each other and help each other become the people the Lord would have us become."[2] As we think of others, we are less likely to feel the need to promote ourselves. Living and thinking modestly are as important as dressing modestly. In the example of Isabella, she could have asked her children if they would respond the same way given a different talent or gift from God. For example, if Isabella's son were very intelligent and got good grades in school, would he wave his paper or test grades around for all his friends to see? "Look at me, I am so smart!" If her daughter were a skilled basketball player, would she tell everyone how wonderful she was by showing off and always trying to one-up her team members? "Look at me, I'm the best basketball player in the school!" Showing off our bodies or using our sexuality just to get attention or to feel more self-worth is similar to bragging about other gifts we have been given. While we do not want to hide our talents and gifts, we can help our children to understand that our bodies and sexuality are not to be put on display and valued for form over function.

While many might think that modesty refers mainly to clothing or sexuality, its real concern is with general worldliness (see

Isaiah 3:16–23; 1 Peter 3:3). Modest dress and appearance are important, but parents can teach the deeper spiritual message that modest thought, modest behavior, and modest sexuality provide protection in our lives. After all, what we are trying to teach our children is to be whole—sexually whole, emotionally whole, and spiritually whole. Sister Carol F. McConkie taught, "How beautiful and how blessed are they who are guided by the Holy Ghost, who protect themselves from worldliness, and who stand as witnesses of God to the world."[3] Parents who teach this broad message of modesty will likely find their children are less influenced by the messages of our popular culture and are more likely to feel peace.

Chapter Highlights

Modesty is really a way of life, not just a standard of dress.

Sexual modesty helps us keep this part of ourselves sacred and strengthens our understanding of our divinity.

We are each responsible for our thoughts and behaviors, and transferring blame undermines our agency.

When we work to be modest in thought, behavior, speech, and dress, we feel greater peace about who we are striving to be.

Thought Questions

What do conversations of modesty look like in your family? How do you think helping a child to be modest about his or her accomplishments relates to modesty of dress?

In your family, are external appearances or accomplishments more valued than genuine interest in others, service for family and friends, or other Christlike attributes? How can a focus on the Savior and becoming like Him help your children to more fully understand the principle of modesty?

Putting It into Practice

Some ideas for children to better practice achieving modesty:

- Don't brag about your accomplishments.
- Try not to show off for the approval of others.
- Share personal accomplishments with only your closest friends and family.
- Avoid talking about material possessions you have.
- Be positive about yourself and don't put yourself down.
- Give others a chance to talk.
- Compliment others.
- Show genuine concern and interest in everyone around you, not just your friends.
- Practice humility.
- Thank people for their help and give credit to others.

Consider choosing one of the ten suggestions for achieving modesty and practicing it as a family for a week. Discuss at family home evening how you did and what thoughts you had about modesty during the week.

Discuss what sexual modesty is. How can we promote sexual modesty without promoting shame or other unhealthy attitudes in sex?

SECTION 3

HELPING YOUR CHILD UNDERSTAND SPECIFIC SEXUAL ISSUES

Chapter 9

Self-Touching and Masturbation

Emphasizing how evil a habit is may be the least effective way to help someone learn to eliminate inappropriate behavior.

This may very well be the chapter that is the most uncomfortable for parents to read but also the most important for giving parents the opportunity to have a positive influence on their children becoming sexually whole. Why is this? Well, masturbation—which is when an individual touches or otherwise stimulates his or her own body to increase sexual arousal—is likely to be one of the first sexual experiences that individuals have in their lives and the most common sexual experience individuals have prior to marriage. Some people find this topic so unnatural that it is quite repulsive to them, and it's even difficult to say the word "masturbation." While we suspect such a strong reaction to the term probably comes from harsh conditioning or shame-based parenting, by approaching the topic in an open way, we are not suggesting that we think masturbation is acceptable or preferable; rather, we are acknowledging that it is common. Consequently, we will teach this topic more directly than it has been addressed in the past, because the mishandling of this issue is one of the primary ways that LDS individuals' sexual development goes awry.

According to Sharon Lamb and Aleksandra Plocha, experts on sexuality during childhood, approximately 40% of girls and 60% of boys masturbate between the ages of two and five, as reported by their mothers. However, because mothers are very likely to underreport this behavior, it is likely that these numbers are much higher in reality. It is safe to say that the majority of young children have masturbated by the time they reach elementary school. We do not have accurate information to present statistics on how common masturbation is among LDS individuals, but we feel confident in saying that most LDS individuals, both male and female, will masturbate in their lifetime. We say this confidently because of our direct experience with thousands of LDS youth and because of our familiarity with national statistics on this issue.

While from one perspective it is as natural to touch erogenous zones of our body (such as our genitals and breasts) as it is to touch our own hand, from a spiritual perspective, we believe and teach that sexual arousal is something we are working hard to restrict to a process that only occurs in marriage. So while our children are very likely at some point to touch their genitals or other body parts and then feel some arousal that leads to touching these body parts repeatedly, we have the goal to help them learn that the sexual arousal process is intended to be shared only between married partners. It is also very natural for partners who are attracted to one another who start kissing and hugging to then desire sexual intercourse. Even so, we do not imply that because it is natural, we should accept that this is what should happen before marriage. Anytime we simply allow whatever physical urges we have to be expressed without thought for future consequences and relational and spiritual goals, we are on a path to distress and unhappiness. This is true for physical hunger, sexual hunger, hunger for recreation, or any other urges we have.

To help parents approach the issue of masturbation, we will present examples of a very young child and a young teenager as they interact with their parents around this issue.

Masturbation during Childhood

Cynthia was a little over four years old and was a very tactile child, meaning that she enjoyed feeling with her skin all sorts of neat things, from soft stuffed animals to the way water felt running over her skin. She would commonly touch other family members and rub their skin, hair, etc., to learn about the physical world around her. We might expect with this high sensitivity and enjoyment of touch that she would start to touch her body all over to explore the sensations and feelings that this aroused. This is exactly what she did, and she discovered that there were strong and powerful feelings associated with touch to her nipples and clitoris, which she started to do repeatedly. Initially her mother and father would notice her hands down her pants and would say to her in a loud voice, "Cynthia, get your hands out of your pants! That is gross! Do you want people to see you with your hands down your pants and make fun of you?" They were not necessarily thinking of this as related to Cynthia's sexual development; they were really thinking of it as the lack of good hygiene and the embarrassment this would bring them and Cynthia in public places. Because they did not take the time to think about the implications and possibility that she was sexually arousing herself, they inadvertently were beginning to develop a pattern of emotions in Cynthia's mind suggesting that sexual feelings were gross and wrong. Of course, a four-year-old has very little impulse control and must learn this slowly over time, but Cynthia did not want to get yelled at and was a relatively compliant child, so she started to touch herself sexually only when she thought her parents would not see her.

Consequently, the first message and associations Cynthia was learning about her sexual self was that the sexual feelings were wonderful and enjoyable but "wrong" and something to be hidden from her mother and father and other people. However, four-year-olds are terrible at hiding things from parents, so over the course of the next few months her parents "caught" her multiple times touching herself in her room, during baths, etc., and started to become alarmed that she had a problem. Like most parents, they simply intensified their current behaviors rather than stepping back and thinking carefully about what to do to help Cynthia begin to develop self-control and healthy sexual attitudes. So when they caught Cynthia masturbating alone they would yell at her, usually startling her and sometimes making her cry, by saying things like, "Cynthia, that is wrong and we don't do that!" Sometimes they would put her in time out. Eventually, with repeated punishment and scolding over more than a year, Cynthia learned to stop touching herself, and her parents were relieved she wasn't doing that "gross thing" anymore and felt good that they had done what was appropriate as parents. While Cynthia stopped the behavior because she was a highly compliant child and one who would have relatively good self-control in her life, many children would not be as compliant as Cynthia without harsher punishments, or they would simply learn to be sneakier and to hide their sexual behaviors. This is a core problem for many youth in the Church, which leaves them with nowhere to talk or discuss sexual feelings and behaviors.

It is crucial here to clarify that whether or not Cynthia or other children stop touching themselves is not the immediate goal. It is an important goal, but it is not the immediate goal parents should be focusing on. If parents get sidetracked into thinking that stopping the touch is the immediate goal, they will lose track of what is most important and feel a false sense of security that they are being successful in teaching their children to be sexually proper and righteous. *This is the fundamental and most common mistake most parents make in the area of teaching children about sexuality: they believe that controlling behavior by instilling in children the idea that something is wrong, sinful, or inappropriate is the goal.* Teaching children that sexual feelings are wrong, sinful, or something to be ashamed about is the exact opposite of what we need to teach and will produce long-term effects that can be devastating. Yet this is exactly what most parents and leaders teach children and youth, primarily and almost exclusively focusing on what children should *not* do with their sexual feelings and thoughts and the bad things that can happen to them if they do not control their behaviors.

Instead, to help their children become sexually whole and enjoy sexuality in its beauty and wonder within marriage, parents will want to instill in children a sense of the beauty and joy that come from sexual feelings and experiences. This can only occur if children learn to accept themselves as sexual beings because their parents have helped them feel this acceptance. So to illustrate this with Cynthia, let's imagine that her parents understood this more important goal and approached the issue of her touching herself differently. Mostly with children who are not very verbal or who are quite young, usually under four, the best approach would be to initially say little if anything about self-touching. Instead, the parents should distract children by giving them something else to do with their hands, such as, "Cynthia, look at this pillow on the couch. Feel how soft and cozy it is?" when they noticed her hand down her pants. This type of distracting would continue consistently until they felt she was old enough to have more of a conversation.

As Cynthia got older, when her parents saw or noticed her touching herself, they would need to understand their own feelings of fear, panic, disgust, or anything else negative they were thinking or feeling. They would need to conquer their own negative feelings first so that they would not bleed over into their interactions with Cynthia. If they thought something like, "That is gross. Why is my daughter so nasty? I never touched myself like that," they would need to talk to themselves and substitute more appropriate thoughts, such as, "No, it is perfectly normal for children to want to touch themselves, so I need to approach this with acceptance and love and not create negative associations of shame or fear with her sexual feelings." Hopefully with this proper understanding they might say to themselves, "My main goal is to help her understand her body and to feel comfortable talking about it with me so we can begin to help her understand what to do with her sexual feelings." So then instead of the harsh "What are you doing? Stop that!" type statements, they will approach the topic with a gentle and calm voice and say something like, "Cynthia, does that feel good?" To her affirmative response, they might reply, "Yes, there are certain parts of our bodies that are very enjoyable to touch. This includes your clitoris and vagina and your nipples. Do you know what these body parts are?" To her response of no, they could then explain, “Your nipples are the rosy-colored parts of your breasts; your vagina and clitoris are the parts of your body between your legs that feel really good to touch” (they might use line drawings of children’s bodies or drawings such as those in Chapter 6 to show her these body parts). They might continue, “Do you know why they feel so good to touch?” Again to her negative response, “God has made certain parts of our bodies so that they feel really good when they are touched. When we are older, this helps us feel that we would like to get married and let our husbands touch us and give us these good feelings. However, God wants us to learn to not touch ourselves or to let anyone else touch us until we are married. This might be a little hard to resist now, because it feels very good, doesn’t it? Sometimes you might not resist, and this does not mean you are bad; it just means it is hard to resist. Please talk to me and I might be able to help you.” Cynthia may then have a variety of questions that would be answered according to her ability to understand.

Masturbation during and after Puberty

The experience and meaning of masturbation changes as children sexually mature. The experience changes because now masturbation is associated with mature sexual anatomy and the stronger hormones and brain chemistry that accompany sexual behaviors. The meaning changes because although their brains are still not fully formed, teenagers have a clearer sense of choice and understanding than young children. According to Devon Hensel and Dennis Fortenberry, experts on sexuality across the life span, by age eighteen approximately 60% of men and 40% of women have masturbated in the last ninety days, and because these are self-report statistics of an embarrassing behavior, it is likely that the rates are much higher. By the middle twenties, 92% of males and 77% of females have masturbated. Again, this means the behavior is common for the majority of both males and females. While we know something about the rates of masturbation, we know much less about the effects of masturbation on mental health, sexual adjustment, and marriage. There are some studies that show weak associations with masturbation and depression and lower sexual adjustment, but these studies often include the effects of pornography also, and so it is difficult to disentangle the two issues.

However, the lack of scientifically proven negative effects for masturbation may not be as relevant for LDS families who are as worried about the spiritual effects as they are about any physical or relational effects. Consequently, because our goal should be to help our children become sexually whole, and this means expressing sexuality exclusively in marriage, we offer the following example as a way to facilitate this goal.

Tom was thirteen. As he sexually matured, his desire to masturbate became intense and seemed almost constant to him. The sexual feelings would fill up his whole body and create a strong feeling of tension and distraction that made it hard to study, not look at girls the wrong way, or do anything else until after he masturbated. While initially his masturbation started rather accidentally in the shower when he noticed strong feelings of excitement as he was cleaning his genitals, recently he would often get aroused by looking at ads for swimsuits in magazines and newspapers. Sometimes he would take one of these into his room and fantasize about the women and masturbate. He knew masturbation was wrong, but he had a very hard time controlling his feelings, and it seemed that the only thing that allowed him to focus on something other than his sexual feelings was to relieve the tension through masturbation. He wanted to talk to his father about his behavior, or maybe even his deacons quorum adviser, but Tom thought of his bishop as a very stern man and he did not think it would go well if he spoke to him. Still, he had not talked to anyone about this because he felt so ashamed and unworthy. His parents had never spoken to him about sex at all, and he had only learned about masturbation being wrong during one of the bishop's Sunday evening youth discussions about the principles in the *For the Strength of Youth.* His bishop had said that touching yourself to become sexually aroused was called masturbation and was very wrong and would lead to evil thoughts and actions that were worse and that masturbation was unworthy of a priesthood holder. Tom felt awful when he first heard his bishop say this, as he had not really thought it was wrong or even wondered about it—he had just enjoyed the feelings. Since the youth discussion, he started to avoid helping with the sacrament when he had masturbated within a few days of Sunday because he felt evil. He felt so bad about himself that he stopped praying on days when he masturbated. He tried really hard to resist the temptation but usually could not go more than a few days without it, and usually after losing control he would just masturbate several times a day for many days until he felt really bad and tried to stop and the cycle would all start again. This had gone on for more than a year, and recently he had just decided he was not going to ever get over this and would probably not be able to go on a mission or do other things that God wanted him to do.

While Tom's behavior is normal and common, he is at a very crucial place as his esteem and spiritual progress are plummeting and he has no place to discuss or deal with this dilemma in a way that would give him the support he needs. On his current course, he is likely to grow more distant from parents, leaders, and God at the very time when he needs their support the most.

As he continues to define himself as sinful, lacking spiritual strength and worthiness, etc., he will naturally want to distance himself from the settings such as church where these feelings of shame are strengthened. This will leave him more vulnerable to the influence of less spiritually-minded friends and to activities such as pornography.

Once an adolescent has a consistent habit of masturbation, it is unlikely that it will simply stop entirely until after many years of struggle and much effort, usually with support from others. Unfortunately, this support and help is not likely to happen unless parents start when children are very young and teach them it is safe and comfortable to talk about sexual feelings and behaviors and that they will not get shamed or punished. However, there are sometimes parents and leaders that can break through this poor conditioning and open up dialogue later in life with children and begin to help youth feel good about themselves and their potential to overcome habits.

If Tom stays connected to his family and faith but is not helped to understand his sexuality and work through his problems with masturbation, he may stumble into marriage with considerable baggage regarding sexuality. He may be able to work through this with a supportive spouse, but he may also remain isolated and feel conflicting feelings about sexuality for much of his life.

So let's imagine that Tom discloses to his father or mother or priesthood leader that he has a problem with masturbation. This would be a very important opportunity to begin to build confidence in him as a normal sexual being who wants to work toward a place where he can control his sexual impulses. The following is an example of what a priesthood leader or parent might say to him as they begin to work together on this issue:

"Tom, I am impressed with your courage at sharing something that can seem very embarrassing and difficult to talk about. This means to me that you are really motivated to change, and I am very hopeful that together, and with God's help, you can begin to work toward a life where you are able to control your sexual impulses.

"I also want to let you know that this behavior does not mean you are evil, perverted, or messed up. It also does not mean that you are unworthy or that God does not love you as much as He did before you had this problem. It simply indicates that you have normal and natural sexual feelings that are difficult to control, and this will be one of your opportunities to grow and learn throughout your life.

"Tom, I want to ask you some additional questions to help me understand the nature of your struggle and the ways we can start to work together to overcome it. Though some questions might be a little embarrassing, it is important that you try and be as honest as you can. This will help you feel better about getting these things out in the open, but more importantly, it will help us develop strategies to begin to control your sexual feelings and behaviors."

At this point, Tom's parent or Church leader might want to ask some questions to help understand when the behavior started, what things exist in his environment that increase his desire to masturbate and have been paired with masturbation, what things he has tried that have helped him have days or hours when it was not as hard to resist masturbation, how his relationship with God and his feelings toward the Church have changed since the behavior started, and so on.

Parents or leaders must control their feelings of shock or dismay at whatever someone might share and work hard to not share these feelings or show them in their reactions. The overriding goal is to help someone like Tom feel that this is one place where it is totally safe to share anything without fearing that he or she will be judged, shamed, or punished.

Beyond the goals of helping Tom feel accepted by God and parents or leaders, that there is hope, and that someone will be on this journey with him, the next most important goal is the process of learning to control habits. Though relatively straightforward, it is not easy to consistently implement. All of us have some habit or tendency that is difficult to keep at the proper level, whether that happens to be resisting sweets, watching excessive TV, losing our patience, or something else. It is helpful to remind ourselves of this as we work with others that have struggles different than our own. And because there are likely to be many times when Tom makes progress and then goes back to old habits, it is crucial that the parent or leader not get frustrated with Tom and give up on him or punish him. Tom will have plenty of these negative feelings on his own, and while it can be frustrating to see someone keep making the same mistakes, we all struggle to be consistent in this world. The purpose of the gospel is to help the sinner stay in the slow and often tedious battle of improvement, not to have unrealistic expectations about being perfect in a short period of time. Elder Jeffrey R. Holland reminded us, "With the gift of the Atonement of Jesus Christ and the strength of heaven to help us, we can improve, and the great thing about the gospel is we get credit for trying, even if we don't always succeed."[1]

The questions Tom's parents (or leader) need to ask him should help him to identify the internal cues he experiences both before and after masturbation and the external cues that help or hinder his desire to stop masturbating. Tom may be hard on himself when he struggles at school or work and then be more vulnerable to letting his guard down. He may be saying very destructive and mean things to himself after masturbating that erode his esteem and lead to more masturbation. He may be watching or spending long periods of time in front of screens that have salacious material. He may have friends who make it difficult for him to be consistent in his gospel practices. He may have an incorrect view of God as a punishing, demanding God who is always unhappy with him. As Tom and his parents begin to understand the processes that lead up to and follow masturbation, they can begin to plan how to intervene earlier, at the first feelings he has that might lead him to masturbate, and thereby give him more space to have barriers in place. Once this information is gathered, action plans and goals can be established and monitored.

It will be useful for Tom and his parents to help him learn to develop other physical activities in life, especially those that require physical discipline, such as exercise, sports, hiking, or hobbies that require physical skill like learning a musical instrument or painting. These positive physical activities can help him learn to be disciplined and have something else to look forward to for releasing tension rather than just sexual release.

Research has shown that when people make goals about controlling appetites, like eating less, exercising more, or controlling sexual urges, and they only think about the possible positive outcomes and focus most of their attention on "being more disciplined," they are very likely to fall back into old habits and not succeed at behavioral change. What seems to happen is that these fantasies about how great it will be when the problem is entirely gone provide some of the immediate neurological awards of dopamine that curiously keep the individual from succeeding in the long run. Also, this typical approach can put too much emphasis on the problem or appetite, which is likely to be lifelong rather than something that is easy to change. A newer approach with the acronym WOOP has shown considerable promise in improving success. The *W* stands for *wish*, or what is the desired goal—in this instance, to reduce or eliminate masturbation. The first *O* stands for what would be the optimal *outcome* of achieving this wish—in this instance, feeling better about one's sexuality or being closer to God or being better prepared for marriage, etc. The next two letters are the most important. The second *O* stands for the typical *obstacles* that someone is likely to encounter inside of him- or herself that will impede success. These might be that when someone gets tired his defenses get weak and he watches things he shouldn't, or he gets bored and thinks about sex too much, or struggles at school and gets upset and depressed, and so on. The *P* stands for the *plan* for improving on the things inside oneself that interfere with success. In the planning process, it is important to develop an if/then scenario that includes the typical obstacles. So if one of Tom's obstacles is that he feels bad when he did not do as well as he wished on school assignments or because he masturbated and then does not want to do anything but surf the Internet, part of his plan might be, "If I feel bad and want to waste time on the Internet, then I will go and call my friend or play basketball so I am with people." This approach is more successful than just hoping to improve and focusing on being more disciplined, because the individual begins to focus on something other than the appetite and on things he or she can practice that are one step removed from the habit he or she is trying to overcome. It also helps the individual not develop an identity that is focused on the habit of masturbation and instead is focused on being more successful at school, or being more consistent about getting regular rest, or being engaged in active hobbies and activities with friends, etc. There are several excellent books by the developer of the WOOP method, Gabriele Oettingen, that might be helpful for parents and adolescents, including *Rethinking Positive Thinking: Inside the New Science of Motivation.*

LDS families have additional resources through the spiritual doctrines embedded in the Atonement. They can add an *S* to the end of the acronym for the Savior, making it WOOPS. Central to the Atonement of Jesus Christ is the concept of change or growth. The idea is that because Christ has paid the weighty costs of sin, we need not beat ourselves up about our mistakes. Rather, we can have hope that by sustaining our focus on Christ and His grace and enduring to the end by struggling against our weaknesses, we will eventually be saved. Unfortunately, so many people in the Church experience their religion as something that increases shame and depression rather than hope and faith. In this regard, it is helpful to consider carefully the principles and doctrines embedded in Ether 12:27: "And if men come unto me I will show unto them their weakness. I give unto men weakness that they may be humble; and my grace is sufficient for all men that humble themselves before me; for if they humble themselves before me, and have faith in me, then will I make weak things become strong unto them."

This scripture can be misinterpreted by some to suggest that a particular sin or habit we have is from God. However, God is not the author of sin, but He has created human beings, and in their fallen, imperfect state they are prone to "weakness," which results in their tendency to make mistakes and sin.

However, this general weakness is supposed to turn them toward God for help and support. So Tom's weakness is not that he masturbates but that he is a human like the rest of us and has a difficult time controlling impulses and appetites and habits. Whenever we struggle with a habit, we should turn to God. He tells us that His grace is sufficient for us all—a wonderful promise. If we turn to God and have faith that He has power to help us grow stronger, we will get help to make small, incremental steps toward improvement and we will hold on to our hope even if we occasionally backslide and make mistakes again. Eventually, and with some of our more persistent struggles perhaps over the course of a lifetime, we will become stronger and find it is much easier to resist our appetites. But if we forget the source of our strength, the grace of God, we may very well be left to our own devices and falter again.

In general conference, Sister Sheri Dew reminded us all of the power of the Atonement and the dangers of relying only on ourselves when she said, "Our responsibility is to learn to draw upon the power of the Atonement. Otherwise we walk through mortality relying solely on our own strength. And to do that is to invite the frustration of failure and to refuse the most resplendent gift in time or eternity."[2]

It is very important that a parent or leader not get into a nattering or pestering mode with Tom and let their entire relationship revolve around whether or not he has resisted his impulses. This problem should be kept in proper perspective as an issue that is not anywhere near as serious as other sexual behaviors such as fornication, and that it will be a temptation for much of his life that should not define his central feelings for himself; his sexuality; his feelings for God, leaders, or parents; or his feelings toward the Church. As his love for parents,

God, and spouse increase over his life, masturbation will lose its allure and become much less attractive and will be seen in the proper light as a poor substitute for a satisfying sexual relationship with a spouse and a barrier to retaining a better relationship with God.

Chapter Highlights

Masturbation is very common for both men and women and for children of all ages.

The way parents intervene to help their children with this problem is often where positive or negative feelings surrounding sexuality develop and persist into adulthood.

Controlling behavior is not as important as developing an open, caring relationship in which sexual feelings and mistakes can be discussed and support can be received.

Distracting young children is often the wisest approach until they are verbal.

Helping older children identify internal and external cues that lead to sexual feelings and thoughts is a good first step.

Thought Questions

Do you feel like you were taught how to manage sexual thoughts and feelings without shame and self-hate?

Do you have confidence you could help your child have a better experience than you had with this area of sexual development?

Do you think your child has or is likely to have a problem in this area? How would you know?

Are you able to help your child find hope through the Atonement of Jesus Christ that changes can be made with persistent, prayerful effort?

Putting It into Practice

Remind yourself and your child of the following:

Our bodies are a gift from Heavenly Father and are wonderful and beautiful.

These strong and powerful sexual feelings will always be a challenge to learn to control.

You should not feel ashamed or bad about having these feelings; they are part of the gifts God has given us to draw us toward our future spouse.

You should not feel evil or bad even if you have a hard time controlling these feelings and sometimes you make mistakes. You should feel disappointed and have a desire to do better next time.

No matter how disappointed you feel, it should never lead you to dislike your sexual feelings, your body, or yourself or feel like you cannot talk to us about your struggles. The purpose of life is to learn to control passions and feelings and direct them in pathways that bring joy. This is what it feels like to be an adult. God understands it is a challenge and will always love you and be willing to help, as will your parents and leaders.

It is worse to feel unworthy and evil and to feel you cannot pray, be involved in church, or have spiritual experiences than it is to make mistakes. This is how the adversary gets us to give up.

The best way to learn to control these feelings and behaviors is to talk openly with us and with your Heavenly Father in prayer and get ideas and support, understand the internal and external cues that increase your desire to masturbate, begin to create barriers between these cues, and keep working at it.

Chapter 10

Pornography

Most pornography problems are more about maturation than they are about addiction.

James and Kelly have noticed that their fourteen-year-old son, Connor, has become increasingly moody and unhappy. Connor had always been their happy-go-lucky boy who talked to his parents about everything. Initially they chalked up his mood shift to typical adjustment issues in the junior high years. Plus, they had recently moved and Connor was still getting situated with new friends and their new neighborhood. However, as the weeks passed, they grew increasingly concerned about Connor's mood and the irritable ways he treated his younger siblings. One night after a heated exchange between Connor and his younger sister, James and Kelly confronted Connor about his recent behavior.

"Connor, what's going on with you?" asked his father.

"What do you mean?" said Connor, still visibly upset about his younger sister coming into his room.

"You seem so upset all the time," his mother added, "is everything OK at school?"

"School is fine," replied Connor.

"What has you so upset?" asked James. "C'mon, bud, you can tell us."

Tears welled up in Connor's eyes. "If I tell you, you'll never look at me the same again."

"What are you talking about?" replied Kelly, trying not to sound too concerned.

"I look at porn and I don't think I can stop," whispered Connor as his emotions overwhelmed him.

Kelly and James were stunned. They didn't let their kids have the Internet on their cell phones, and they kept their home computer in the family room. *How could this happen to our kid?* They then listened to Connor as he told them about how he had been accessing pornography since he was twelve years old through social media sites on his cell phone even without an Internet browser. They wondered what their next steps should be. Does Connor have an addiction? Does he need a therapist? Is this normal behavior? How should they handle this as parents?

Situations like Connor's are becoming increasingly common among our children these days. But despite the fact that pornography is becoming a common part of our modern culture, most parents still feel ill-equipped to handle these situations when they come up with their children. Sometimes children will voluntarily share their struggles with their parents or priesthood leaders, like Connor did with his parents. But often pornography use is discovered by the parents on a computer or phone, or parents catch their son or daughter using porn or start to have suspicions about his or her media use patterns. Some teens have observable changes in their mood or behaviors, while others get involved with pornography and view it for some time with no recognizable shifts in their demeanor.

In this chapter, we discuss some guiding principles for how to safeguard your children from pornography and how to respond when a child is exposed to or becomes involved with pornography. In particular, we suggest five proactive strategies we can use to help address the issue of pornography in our homes and in our children's lives. These include (1) learning about pornography, (2) preventing early exposure, (3) replacing myth with truth, (4) diagnosing the problem correctly, and (5) being patient and fostering long-term change.

Learning about Pornography

Many parents wonder, "Just how big of a problem is pornography?" A few years ago, our team of researchers at BYU published a highly publicized study in the *Journal of Adolescent Research* entitled "Generation XXX: Pornography Use and Acceptance among Emerging Adults." In this study, we documented how prevalent pornography use has become among young adults in the United States. The clear finding from our study was that pornography has moved from the fringe to the mainstream of society. Specifically, we found that 87% of young adult men ages eighteen to twenty-five reported viewing online pornography within the last twelve months and that 50% said they viewed it on at least a weekly basis. Our study also found that 30% of young adult women had viewed or read pornographic material in the last year and that half of the women we sampled believed that viewing pornography was an acceptable way for someone to express their sexuality.

Naturally, these patterns are alarming to us as parents and leaders who are becoming increasingly concerned about the pornographic culture that is emerging in modern society. This alarm has been growing for some time now, and we have been steadily raising the voice of warning about pornography to our young people. In fact, we are now getting to the point where nearly all of our young adults are raised from childhood with repeated warnings about the negative consequences of pornography. When our team first coined the phrase "Generation XXX" we used the term to refer to young people getting directly involved with pornography, but now we believe that "Generation XXX" may be an apt title for all of today's young people—they are all a part of the pornography generation, whether they personally use pornography or not. They have all been greatly impacted by the warnings about pornography they have repeatedly received from parents, ward leaders, seminary teachers, and others.

Now that we are more than several decades past the emergence of the Internet, what are the consequences of our collective warnings about pornography to our children? Have we been effective? Are we helping our children successfully avoid the pornography pitfalls in our society? As researchers, we are becoming increasingly convinced that our collective voice of warning about pornography has brought *mixed results* in the rising generation. On the positive side, nearly all of the teens and young adults in the Church see pornography as a serious matter. Rarely do we hear anyone try to dismiss or minimize the potential negative impacts of pornography involvement. We can safely conclude that the awareness level of the "pornography problem" is very high.

However, we have also come to believe that the warnings young people are receiving from their parents and leaders about pornography are often leading to some unintended negative side effects. These side effects are not necessarily a result of the fact that we are warning our children about pornography but rather are a result of *how* we are warning them. Also, while a few of these side effects are the result of what parents are saying about pornography, many of the biggest problems are the result of what we are *not* talking about—specifically, healthy sexuality and natural sexual development. Too many teens and young adults are learning about pornography in unspecific and isolated ways.

While it is debatable whether or not our warnings about pornography and sexual permissiveness have changed the overall behaviors of teens and young adults in the Church, it is clear they have influenced young people's feelings about sex. And while young men have primarily been the ones targeted by these messages, it is clear that it is our young women who are paying the most attention. And what have they heard? They have heard that they should be very concerned about pornography use among young men and how it can impact their future marriage one day.

The key problem is that this concern about pornography isn't just about pornography. It's about sex altogether. The message that has been received is, "Porn is bad and porn is sex, so sex is bad." Why would our young people believe this? Because for many of them, teachings about pornography have not been integrated into a broader understanding of sexuality. In their experience, pornography was what was talked about—not healthy sexuality, not the beauty of sexual intimacy between spouses, not an understanding of how their body is endowed with a powerful sexual response system. As a parent, the best thing you can do to safeguard your children from ongoing struggles with pornography is to raise them with an understanding of their sexual nature and ways that pornography undermines their potential for sexual wholeness in marriage one day. In reference to pornography and other inappropriate expressions of sexuality, Elder Jeffrey R. Holland explained, "If we stop chopping at the branches of this problem and strike more directly at the root of the tree, not surprisingly we find lust lurking furtively there. . . . Why is lust such a deadly sin? Well, in addition to the completely Spirit-destroying impact it has upon our souls, I think it is a sin because it defiles the highest and holiest relationship God gives us in mortality—the love that a man and a woman have for each other and the desire that couple has to bring children into a family intended to be forever."[1]

Preventing Early Exposure

As parents, we naturally want to protect our children from harmful experiences. So it is natural to ask the question, "Can we prevent our children from seeing pornography?" The answer to this question is yes and no. We say "yes and no" not because we are uncertain or wishy-washy about this question but rather to acknowledge the developmental reality of this question. Remember our discussion of pre-arming versus cocooning in Chapter 3. Pornography is a prime example of a problem that is best addressed through pre-arming rather than cocooning. Safeguarding our children from pornography involves what parenting experts call "external monitoring" and "internal monitoring." *External monitoring* involves parents restricting access and setting limits—which is more effective with younger children. *Internal monitoring* is a key component of the pre-arming strategy of proactive parenting and involves teaching our children *why* a certain behavior is not good for them and helping them be prepared to regulate themselves when they are confronted with temptation. With the prevalence of pornography in our culture, we need to developmentally transition from a strategy of external monitoring of our younger children to fostering a readiness for internal monitoring in our teens and young adult children.

External Monitoring—Limiting Access to Pornography

It has been reported that as many as 90% of children ages eight to sixteen years old have viewed pornography online, and in many cases this exposure was unintentional. Today, with 95% of teens using the Internet, pornography has never been easier for kids to access, and studies document the average age of first exposure at about twelve years old. We have also moved into the era of "pocket porn," when many of our children are accessing pornography through smartphones and tablet devices. In the United States, over 75% of teens have a cell phone, and kids are getting access to pornography that their parents are not even aware is happening.

While many of these trends highlight the growing need for pre-arming our children to make good choices on their own and turn away from pornographic media, they should not deter us from making every effort we can to prevent our children from encountering pornography for as long as possible. Research suggests that the longer our children can avoid their first exposure to pornographic material, the more prepared developmentally they will be to process and deal with what they eventually see. Postponing pornography exposure is not only helpful in diminishing the chance of unhealthy habits and obsessive use, but it also allows for healthy sexual development to occur. We need to do all we can to safeguard our children until they can safeguard themselves.

A few simple steps and reasonable rules can protect children from unintentional exposure and help them thoughtfully consider the content they choose to view online. These include (1) using filters (at the computer, router, and even Internet-service-provider levels), (2) keeping computers in common areas—particularly outside of children's bedrooms (including laptops), (3) having kids turn in their electronic devices at night, (4) setting parental controls on device access, and (5) having an "open-book policy" in which parents can read texts and social media posts at any time. There have been a number of Internet accountability software programs developed in recent years that parents can install on their home computers and family members' cell phones. Accountability programs are proving particularly useful because rather than trying to filter content they maintain a record of all of the images that appear on a computer or phone screen. This approach avoids the inconsistencies of many filter programs and provides parents with a viewing record from all family members' devices that is not erasable on a computer history.

It bears mentioning that we need to safeguard our daughters as much as we do our sons from exposure to pornography. Newer research suggests that pornography use is increasing among teen girls and young adult women—including in LDS circles. The pornography industry is intentionally trying to recruit more female users by creating pornography with more narrative content and story lines to attract women. Too many parents and youth leaders are labeling pornography as a "young men's problem"—leaving our daughters exposed to pornography without direct prevention and help when exposure occurs. Because of this lack of discussion, many young women feel particularly intense feelings of shame and embarrassment connected to their pornography use, which in time can become shame about their overall sexuality.

Internal Monitoring—Replacing Myth with Truth

Pre-arming our children is fundamentally about helping them come to see pornography for what it really is and deciding for themselves that it is not how they want to express their sexuality. To do this, we must teach our children about pornography in the context of teaching them about healthy sexuality and the possibility for sexual wholeness in marriage. Only within this context can we help our children come to see how pornography plays on their divinely created desires for sex and counterfeits their desires for love in a real marriage. Of course, marriage is pretty far down the road for a twelve-year-old, but helping our children see that there are healthy and appropriate ways to express their sexuality that are undermined and misdirected by pornography will help them in time come to see pornography for what it really is.

The effects of pornography are best understood in the context of how it disrupts healthy relationship development. In developmentally appropriate ways, we need to help our teen and young adult children understand that having a lasting marriage someday is all about having the *right kind* of relationship. Researchers and therapists have found that marriages that last have *two important bonds* or types of connections in their relationship—a strong *emotional bond* as well as a strong *physical bond* between the two spouses.

The emotional bond is made up of two key parts—love and trust. *Love* stays strong when two people truly care about each other and love each other as whole people—both inside and out. We need to help our children learn that lasting love happens when we choose to love someone with both his or her strengths and weaknesses. *Trust* is built on honesty and truth. When partners stay committed and faithful to each other and share their whole lives with each other, they can build a sense of trust and confidence with each other. When two people really commit to each other, it is easier to feel safe and believe that the relationship is going to last. This helps them be vulnerable with each other and open up their deepest feelings.

Researchers have also found that couples who stay together have a strong physical bond between the partners. An important part of a couple's physical bond is *attraction.* Everyone wants to feel attractive and hopes that his or her spouse one day will be physically attracted to him or her. This is what makes having a boyfriend or girlfriend, or one day a spouse, feel different than having friends or being loved by your mom! Romantic relationships are supposed to be romantic—and having a spark of attraction is a big part of creating a romantic relationship that lasts.

So why does teaching our children about the needed emotional and physical bonds of healthy relationships help with avoiding pornography? Because the truth is that porn undermines real love! And it does so by eroding these key relationship bonds—the emotional bond and the physical bond between spouses. How does pornography do this? Pornography can harm our children in *three main ways* that hurt their chances of having a loving and lasting marriage in the future.

1. Unrealistic expectations. First, porn teaches our children myths about sex, people's bodies, and relationships. Simply put, porn is a really bad form of sex education. Our children get tricked into believing that when they see pornography, they are watching real experiences with real couples, when they are actually seeing a staged, choreographed presentation with people who are strangers to each other. Pornography is not like a real relationship at all. We need to help our children understand that if they use pornography they will likely develop *unrealistic expectations* about what their future romantic relationships and marriage will be like.

Plus, pornography encourages objectification. *Objectification* means treating a person as a thing or object, without regard to his or her thoughts or feelings. We can help our children see that they are objectifying others when they (1) think or talk about others' body parts, (2) treat others as a tool or object for making themselves feel good, (3) treat others as if they are replaceable and don't mean anything to them, (4) believe it is OK to hurt or mistreat others, or (5) believe there is no need for them to worry about the feelings and preferences of others. These five characteristics of objectification are a laundry list of what pornography portrays about sex. Pornography teaches that both men and women aren't worth anything more than the sum of their body parts and how much physical pleasure they can offer. Whether pornography users like it or not, those perceptions often start creeping into how they see themselves and other people in real life. The harder it becomes for the user to see themselves and others as anything more than sexual objects, the harder it is to develop real relationships.

2. Keeping secrets. A second way that we need to help our children realize how pornography harms relationships is that it often happens in secret. Users of pornography typically hide, or at least minimize, their use of pornography from everyone, including their dating partners and spouses. Studies have found that when people engage in this type of "self-concealment"—which is when they do things they are not proud of and keep them a secret from their friends and family members—it not only hurts their relationships and leaves them feeling lonely but also makes them more vulnerable to depression, poor self-esteem, and anxiety.

Keeping secrets damages trust. When spouses keep secrets from each other, their trust in each other erodes and their confidence in their relationships starts to struggle. Studies with women who are spouses or romantic partners of habitual pornography users have found that they feel they "can't trust" their partner and worry about whether he will be faithful to their relationship. On top of creating secrecy in the relationship, pornography also creates expectations and behaviors that place it on a collision course with commitment and exclusivity in the relationship. Research studies have found that people who use pornography are more accepting of cheating on their partners. It is not surprising, then, that the deterioration of trust is the most significant negative impact of pornography use. When teens are getting involved with pornography they rarely think about these types of long-term consequences that can result if they persist in hiding pornography use.

3. Distorted attraction template. Parents should also help their older children understand that a third way that pornography harms relationships is that it distorts what scientists call our "attraction template." Our attraction template is our personal preferences for who we find physically attractive and what types of behaviors we find sexually exciting. *In terms our kids can understand, it is who we find attractive and what turns us on.* Although some people think we simply "have" these preferences, scientists are discovering that we "develop" and "learn" these preferences—and what we look at and watch can shape who and what we are attracted to.

This is where the fantasy and myth of pornography become a big problem. Not only does pornography offer a fictional version of sex education, but also that education is being delivered in a way perfectly tailored to how our brains learn. Images are an especially powerful teacher, since they can pack in a whole lot of information that the viewer can understand very quickly. And while words are often interpreted as opinions, our brains are more likely to interpret images as facts; after all, it's a lot harder to argue with something you're seeing happen in front of you. Our brains also learn better when we are paying close attention and are aroused. When you add in the focused concentration of searching through pornographic images to find exactly what the user is looking for and reinforcing what is being taught with physical pleasure, it creates the perfect conditions for building new beliefs and behaviors.

As a result, users who grow up on porn train their sexuality by looking at virtual images of unrealistic, surgically-altered bodies. Instead of learning to build relationships with real people, it often feels more natural and arousing to them to be alone in front of a computer. Of course, this erodes the level of attraction in a real romantic relationship. Leading relationship experts Drs. John and Julie Gottman have expressed serious concern about the effects of pornography on couple relationships. They explain, "Pornography may be just such a supernormal stimulus. With pornography use, much more of a normal stimulus may eventually be needed to achieve the response a supernormal stimulus evokes. In contrast, ordinary levels of the stimulus are no longer interesting. This may be how normal sex becomes much less interesting for porn users. The data supports this conclusion. In fact, use of pornography by one partner leads the couple to have far less sex and ultimately reduces relationship satisfaction."

Diagnosing the Problem Correctly

Most discussions of pornography today involve some mention of addiction. While this type of warning has heightened our awareness of the ways that pornography use can become habit-forming or obsessive in someone's life, parents should be careful to not confuse the *possibility* of addiction with the *assumption* of addiction. Both experts and Church leaders have pointed out that while some individuals can become addicted to pornography, the majority of pornography users are not addicted. President Dallin H. Oaks recently taught, "Not everyone who uses pornography willfully is addicted to it. In fact most young men and young women who struggle with pornography are not addicted." He went on to say, "That is a very important distinction to make—not just for parents, spouses, and leaders who desire to help but also for those who struggle with this problem. . . . If a behavior is incorrectly classified as an addiction, the user may think he or she has lost agency and capacity to overcome the problem. . . . Having a better understanding of where a person is in the process will also allow a better understanding of what action is necessary to recover."[2]

All of our children experience the power of the sexual response triggered during puberty long before they have the full emotional or spiritual maturity to make sense of it. But if we move too quickly and assume that any involvement with pornography is an addiction, we actually are going to shut down our ability to have openness and dialogue, and often the problem goes unaddressed for several years.

Levels of Involvement

How do you know if your child has a pornography addiction? First, true addiction to pornography is quite rare in teens and more of a possibility in adults who have had years of obsessive use. The answer to this question is complex and differs for each person. Everyone's history, level of use, and degree of dependency with pornography is different—simply put, it's different for everyone. The other thing that is tricky with answering this question is that we tend to think about addiction like a light switch that is either on or off—thus we think someone is either "addicted" or they're not. But habit-forming behavior isn't like a basic light switch that only turns on or off. Rather, it is more like a dimmer switch that gradually changes from light to dark and back again. In short, habits differ by degree, not by kind.

Let's talk about a child's brain for a moment. The brain is involved in every decision our children make—good or bad. The key to their success in overcoming unwanted habits is in learning how to train and direct the brain so that it helps them repeatedly make the choices they (and you) desire most. Think about your children and the sometimes frustrating process they go through when learning their first simple skills: their tiny fingers struggling to tie their shoes or write their name for the first time. As parents we anxiously watched as our child wobbled on a bicycle down the sidewalk. At first, these tasks are difficult and time-consuming. But with practice, the tasks get easier and easier until something almost magical happens—they don't have to think about it anymore; it becomes seemingly natural and automatic. Your child has created a habit.

Now back to the question, "How do you know if your child has an addiction?" As a parent, when you understand how your child's habits are formed, the question is better asked: "How deep of a habit has my child formed?" There are two primary things to consider as you try to answer this question—your child's behaviors and his or her motivations. With behavior, how frequently does your child look at pornography? Is it every day or only once in a while? For how long has he or she looked at pornography? Has it been for three years or three months? With motivations, why does your child look at pornography? What brings him or her back to looking at pornography? When you consider these questions, it might be helpful to think about three levels of habits:

Level 1: A bad habit. The first level we call a "bad habit." Almost everyone has a bad habit or two that they struggle to stop doing. In fact, most New Year's resolutions are about people wanting to change a pattern that is not working for them in life. Some people bite their fingernails, and other people keep checking their cell phone while they are driving. Other people gossip about others even when they have told themselves they are going to stop, and others let their bedrooms get messy even though they swore the last time they cleaned their room it was going to stay that way! Most bad habits don't happen every day, and sometimes people go for weeks or months without engaging in their bad habit—but in time they go back to it, even when they don't want to.

One of the main motivations for viewing pornography that tends to go along with children who have a bad habit is *curiosity*. Remember that it is very natural for our children to be curious about their bodies, the bodies of others, and human sexuality in general—they are naturally interested in sex. In many cases, experiences with pornography, masturbation, and other sexual outlets start out motivated by simple curiosity. Maybe your children were exposed to pornography by accident, through their own efforts, or through friends and family members. In any case, it's usually a natural curiosity that lured them in. After the initial discovery, many teens start using pornography "occasionally." That is, they find it *exciting and arousing.* It's a very convenient and powerful way to feel pleasure, to cope with boredom or mental burnout. In fact, pornography viewing and other unwanted sexual outlets mimic real sexual intimacy by making them feel good for a little while. Most bad habits start out with these motivations. The WOOPS principles presented in the previous chapter can help with addressing habits and making spiritual progress.

Level 2: An obsessive habit. The second level we call an "obsessive habit." Obsessive habits are negative patterns that people engage in on a much more regular basis—sometimes every day. People think about obsessions much more than bad habits and even become a bit compulsive about making sure they happen. Some people oversleep almost every day, and others play video games so much that they are always late to work or don't get their work done. Others want an escape from life struggles and binge watch entire seasons of TV shows in a day or two. Obsessive habits also become more about managing emotions, and people turn to their obsessions to manage stress, depression, or loneliness. Pornography and other unwanted sexual outlets often start out being about the curiosity and excitement. What starts out as recreational use can lead to an escalating form of self-medication that is as much about seeking an escape as it is feeling a rush or a high. Over time, people can start to look for stimulation and think about when they can look at pornography again. People with obsessions start to develop triggers or cues that cause them to start thinking about their habit.

Level 3: An addictive habit. The third level we call an "addictive habit." The main difference between an addictive habit and an obsessive habit is that the person is becoming dependent on the behavior. He or she develops a tolerance that invites them to escalate the habit to higher and higher levels to experience similar feelings. Addiction is a lifestyle, and people with this level of habit-formed behavior start to change other aspects of their life to fit in their habit. When pleasure is easily and instantly accessible, can be produced on demand, and is experienced repetitively—for example, Internet pornography coupled with masturbation—it can become addictive in time. If your children repeatedly use sexual outlets as their primary strategy for pleasure, escape, and coping, they begin to believe, in time, that this is the way to deal with the stresses of life. They can get to the point where sexual outlets and behaviors become a central focus in their life. Their thoughts become dominated by excessive sexual images, urges, and fantasies. Increasing amounts of time, effort, and energy are expended on pursing their habit.

Only you as a parent can judge where your child is on the habit-forming spectrum. But whether you feel your child has a bad habit or if you are sure it's a full-blown addiction, addressing the issue directly and compassionately will help. If you feel your child has a bad habit, then teaching him or her about the harms of pornography and the benefits of healthy sexuality can prevent the pattern from getting worse and out of control. If you suspect that it is an obsession or addiction, then it may be helpful to get some outside help from a trained and experienced professional.

Be Patient and Focus on Long-Term Patterns

In Latter-day Saint culture, there are some aspects of the gospel in which we tend to acknowledge the process of progression, and there are others in which we seem to acknowledge only perfection. In relation to pornography, we rarely hear about a maturation process. All of our children, just like each of us, will learn through some trial and error in their sexual development. It may not be the same for every person, but each of us has some maturity to gain in this part of life. Keeping this maturation perspective in mind is particularly needed when addressing pornography issues among teens and young adults. As Dr. Mark Butler, an expert in pornography treatment, has stated, "The adolescent brain is not fully formed, and that leads to certain issues like impulse control and lack of forward thinking. . . . A spiritually sincere, striving teen can become crippled by overwhelming guilt when he encounters weaknesses that he is uniquely vulnerable to having with that still-adolescent brain. It is so critical that, alongside teaching the commandments, you teach adolescents the Atonement—that it's there for the purpose of developmental patience in life."

Beyond natural curiosity, children often turn to pornography out of an inability to effectively cope with life stress and negative emotions. If this is the case, then children may need some help with identifying triggers and disrupting the patterns they follow when they become depressed, anxious, or stressed. There are a number of things you can do to help your child develop better coping skills. First, teach your child that both positive and negative emotions are a part of everyday life and that it is normal to occasionally experience negative feelings such as sadness, anger, frustration, or hurt. You can also encourage your child to take proactive steps to solve the problems contributing to stress and, when possible and appropriate, reduce your demands on your child. Therapists and counselors teach that as parents we should help our children develop effective approaches to managing stress in their lives, such as talking with close family and friends, exercising, listening to positive music, and spiritual practices like prayer, scripture study, and service.

Although it will be natural for our children to feel guilt after viewing pornography, we should be careful not to shame our children about what they have done. Therapists have long distinguished between guilt and shame. Guilt is a recognition by our child that his or her *behavior* is wrong and is not in harmony with his or her values. Guilt is a natural and normal part of growing up and a healthy response to poor choices that can help motivate needed changes in our child's life. Shame, on the other hand, is when our child focuses on himself or herself *as a bad person* and diminishes his or her sense of self-worth—which discourages hope for change and doesn't motivate change. As parents, we need to be careful not to exacerbate feelings of shame in our children. As they experience our positive support, they will feel more hope that they can learn from their mistakes and make positive changes in their lives.

Chapter Highlights

Children need to learn about the harms of pornography in the context of a broader understanding of healthy sexuality. Young people are more likely to make good decisions about viewing pornography when they understand the specific ways that pornography harms the emotional, physical, and spiritual foundations of sexual wholeness.

Pornography use is best addressed as a topic of progression rather than a topic of perfection. All of our children, just like each of us, will learn through some trial and error in their sexual development. It may not be the same for every person, but each of us has some maturity to gain in this part of life. Keeping this maturation perspective in mind is particularly needed when addressing pornography issues among teens and young adults.

Thought Questions

What is your response to this chapter on pornography use? Do you feel perhaps you need to rethink how you have responded to pornography use in the past?

Have you talked with your children about pornography use, and if so, do you feel there is more you can do or something you might do differently?

If your child has had issues with pornography, which of the levels do you feel his or her behavior fits? How does this approach change the way you think about involvement in pornography?

Putting It into Practice

With younger children, watch the Church's video about pornography (http://overcomingpornography.org/spouses-and-families/what-do-i-do?lang=eng). Use this video to have a conversation about what pornography is and why it is natural for each of us to be curious about and attracted to pornography. Let your children know that you are open and comfortable with talking to them about this topic and would like them to let you know if they see any media like this.

With older children, read President Oaks's *Ensign* article "Recovering from the Trap of Pornography" (October 2015) together. Discuss the levels of pornography involvement and how bad habits can be developed that are not necessarily addiction. Discuss how pornography counterfeits real intimacy and can create unrealistic expectations about sex, people's bodies, and relationships.

Spend some time reviewing the material on the Church's pornography resource website, overcomingpornography.org. The more you learn about the topic, the better resource you can be to your family and others.

Chapter 11

Same-Sex Attraction

"Come unto me, all ye that labour and are heavy laden, and I will give you rest" (Matthew 11:28).

If you want to get LDS parents tied up in knots, start asking them questions about what they would do if their child were attracted to people of the same sex. They will often be tied up in knots because their emotions will be so intense, especially their fears, that it will be hard for them to discuss the issues. There has been so much attention given to this topic in the last decade that most of us have had many opportunities to reflect on how we think and feel about same-sex attraction and how we would feel if one of our own children had feelings of same-sex attraction. Oddly, though, we have rarely found parents who have talked about this issue much at all with their own children. Rather than discussing this important issue in our families and preparing our children to be able to cope with feelings of sexual attraction to others or to be able to discuss this topic with friends and others who do not believe the same things they do, our children are left without our assistance or guidance. Inevitably the primary fear parents have about discussing same-sex attraction with their children is that it will plant ideas in their heads that will germinate into anxiety and maybe even experimentation regarding homosexual thoughts and actions. This is a rather irrational fear, because it is unlikely that parents will discuss anything with their children regarding these issues that the children have not already heard or thought of many times.

As children sexually mature and see their peers doing the same, it is natural and common for there to be some questions, confusion, fear, and difficulty around the issue of sexual orientation. As children of faith, they have been taught that their goals are to be married and have children in a heterosexual relationship, but they see peers and people around them who are homosexual, and they naturally begin to ponder whether they or someone close to them might be gay. This is upsetting to them because they know that a homosexual life would be contrary to their beliefs and could make their goals seem unachievable. It is especially upsetting to them in the context of a culture that has often been teaching that sexual orientation is purely an issue of biological inevitability, that to resist sexual attraction to someone, whether of the same or the opposite sex, is repressive and wrong, and that those who believe otherwise are as evil as those who treated people of different races as inferior and enslaved them. Hence youth of faith are often quite anxious about this issue, so they try not to think about it in an environment that is always talking about it. This is a recipe for unnecessary anxiety, frustration, fear, and desperation. So let's briefly lay out what is known at this point regarding sexual orientation both from a religious perspective and a scientific perspective. Our prophetic leaders have taught us that feelings of sexual attraction are not sinful; only sexual actions outside of heterosexual marriage are sinful: "It's important to remember a few things that people don't always understand or remember. And that is that homosexual behavior is not the unforgivable sin. The Atonement and repentance can bring full forgiveness and peace. And secondly, I'd say though we don't know everything we know enough to be able to say that same-sex attraction in and of itself is not a sin. The feeling, the desire is not classified the same as homosexual behavior itself. And the third point I would mention is that when people have those desires and same-sex attractions, our attitude is, 'Stay with us.' I think that's what God is saying. 'Stay with me.'"[1]

According to Michael Bailey, professor of psychology at Northwestern University, Lisa Diamond, professor of human development at the University of Utah, and others, we learn that close to 95% of individuals can expect to be primarily attracted to individuals of the opposite sex. We also know that most males and about half of females who are attracted to individuals of the same sex have been exclusively that way since they sexually matured and are not likely to change who they are primarily attracted to. About half of females who have ever felt feelings of same-sex attraction and a smaller percentage of males have more fluid feelings of attraction in that sometimes they feel attracted to the same sex and at other times find themselves attracted to someone of the opposite sex. A small percentage of both males and females have very little if any feelings of sexual attraction to anyone of any gender.

Here are some additional things we have learned from science that can dispel myths many still hold about sexual orientation: Marrying someone of the opposite sex will not "cure" someone of same-sex attraction. If an individual with homosexual feelings does marry someone of the opposite sex, he or she can perform sexually and enjoy, to a degree, the physical side of the relationship, though the individual will likely still feel attracted to members of the same sex. There is no clear evidence that sexual abuse during childhood by a perpetrator of the same sex causes same-sex attraction. Masturbation and/or pornography do not affect same-sex attraction. Bad relationship experiences with someone of the opposite sex do not cause people to switch orientations. Poor parenting is not a cause of same-sex attraction. Because of how both males and females are portrayed in the media as sexual objects, but especially females, it is not uncommon for people to feel sexual arousal when viewing these depictions in the media even if the individuals are the same sex as the viewer. Consequently, feeling sexually aroused on occasion by someone of the same sex portrayed in the media is not a reliable indicator that someone is primarily attracted to the same sex.

The most recent research on sexual attraction by Dr. Lisa Diamond and others suggests that it is more fluid than we have thought in the past for some people, especially females. While still a relatively small percentage of females, usually less than three percent, it is an important perspective to consider on sexual attraction. As stated earlier, proportionally more men than women have felt primarily and exclusively attracted to people of the same sex, and there are a significant number of men and even more women who feel sexual attraction to someone of either sex. These fluid individuals seem to have their feelings of sexual attraction trigged by close relationships rather than the gender of the partner. This research on sexual attraction fluidity also shows that the stability of preferences for one gender or another may not be high for some people. So the old ideas of a person who has any tendencies whatever toward same-sex attraction rather quickly and permanently being attracted to only one gender is not supported by the research. *However, this does not mean that people can freely choose whom they are attracted to.* For some people, sexual attraction is more nuanced and complicated than our simple categories of heterosexual and homosexual, but this is different than saying people decide whom they are attracted to. Finally, especially for individuals with more fluid feelings of sexual attraction, because their feelings of sexual attraction seem to be triggered by the closeness of the relationship, their feelings may not solidify toward one sex or the other during adolescence or adulthood; rather, these feelings will simply occur when in a close relationship with someone of either sex. This information should help parents approach conversations and issues about sexual orientation with less anxiety and more accurate information, especially since same-sex attraction is relatively rare as reported by the most scientific research.

If parents have already established an environment where it is safe to talk about sexual matters, children may naturally bring up questions and concerns they have about sexual orientation. If children never bring this up, it is likely they feel embarrassed about it and parents may need to take the opportunity during the many instances of same-sex relationships portrayed in the media to initiate discussions about sexual orientation. Of course, pestering children with a bunch of questions all at once is counterproductive, but a few questions on a regular basis will show your children that you are comfortable talking about sexual orientation and that it is a topic you expect to talk about in your family. As the comfort level increases, it would not be unusual for a child to ask something like, "So how does someone know that they are gay or not?" A parent's anxiety might raise a bit from such a question, but it can relieve the pressure to discuss not prematurely making a decision about whether someone is going to be attracted to same-sex partners or opposite-sex partners. It is helpful to discuss with children that for some people sexual attraction might ebb and flow and that figuring out whether this attraction will settle on one or both genders make take years.

Clarifying that it may not be clear to individuals for a number of years, if ever, how strong their feelings of sexual attraction are, and what type of people they are primarily going to be attracted to, can give children permission to relax and let themselves mature and develop without pressure. There is no rush to decide anything about what feelings of sexual attraction mean until children are at a point where they are starting to date and trying to decide about marriage. Letting children know what God's expectations are regarding sexual behaviors and that both you and God will love them regardless of their feelings of attraction and behaviors is crucial for keeping communication open and accepting. President Dallin H. Oaks reminded us, "The effect of God's commandments and laws is not changed to accommodate popular behavior or desires. If anyone thinks that godly or parental love for an individual grants the loved one license to disobey the law, he or she does not understand either love or law." He continued to discuss how parents should respond to children who are struggling with moral issues and said, "These teachings require continued loving concern, which surely requires continued loving associations."[2]

If it becomes clear over time that one of your children is primarily attracted to individuals of the same sex, this feeling of acceptance by you and God will continue to be crucial in his or her attempts to withstand the strong cultural messages that people must blindly follow and give in to whatever sexual feelings they have regardless of what will make them happiest in the long term. Beyond acceptance, helping children fully understand themselves and encouraging them to be honest about their sexual attraction in their future relationships is crucial. While many people who feel attracted to the same sex and who decide to live consistent with God's commands may not marry a heterosexual partner, a few might, but they should be very clear with potential partners about their feelings of attraction and not pretend they will change just because they get married. Potential partners will need to understand there is a loss in the ideal that they deserve—that is, the ideal of having someone strongly sexually attracted to them—and this should not be taken lightly as something that can be easily dealt with. If both partners still choose to marry, they will need strong support and help to work through this loss, especially in the context where others will think that the decision to marry is offensive and wrong, both within and outside the Church, but for different reasons.

Frankly, most parents and children know far before they are willing to admit that a particular child is attracted to people of the same sex. However, because parents are not willing to talk about it and both parents and their child might have unnecessary feelings of shame, there are often years of delay in fully facing these issues, and then sexual behavioral mistakes are sometimes made that can be very difficult to overcome, only adding to the shame and distance from the Spirit. In addition, without dialogue and support, feelings of guilt and shame can easily turn into feelings of worthlessness, and it is clear that without very strong support, religious individuals struggling with homosexual feelings are at much higher risk for suicide than others. Typically by the early twenties, except for some females and males discussed earlier who are likely to have a more fluid attraction to both sexes, sexual orientation is quite stable. So if during early adolescence just having permission and encouragement to talk about sexual orientation occurs, this will facilitate the more difficult discussions that need to occur by late adolescence in which both parents and children need to be more direct about what will likely be enduring patterns of sexual attraction. As they admit these enduring patterns, they can move beyond the question of whether a particular person is going to be consistently attracted to the same sex and instead move to specific strategies regarding the implications of same-sex attraction for marriage and dating decisions, missions, and so on.

In all instances, parents or children should not be deluded into thinking that by some miracle God is likely to remove feelings of same-sex attraction if enough prayer and fasting are exerted. While we do not doubt that this could happen on very rare occasions, as with any challenge in life, God almost always helps us cope with the challenge but does not take it away from us. Indeed, in a recent story about a mother who painstakingly helped her son through struggles with homosexuality and activity in the Church, it was concluded, "And, I must say, this son's sexual orientation did not somehow miraculously change—no one assumed it would. But little by little, his heart changed."[3] Throughout this process, parents may need to take a more direct role with running interference between leaders and others who are trying to be helpful. While it would be nice to believe that all leaders understand these complex issues and will be appropriately supportive of both keeping the commandments and accepting people for who they are, this is very unrealistic and unsafe when dealing with such a charged issue as sexual orientation. Often individuals who want to be helpful are primarily acting out of their own agendas, whether to help others accept or embrace homosexual relationships for themselves, or convince them they can switch orientations, or teach them how to repent of their "wicked desires," or verify assumptions they have such as the idea that abuse causes homosexuality, or something else. People with these agendas are more likely to be harmful than helpful. In particular, with priesthood leaders who are in roles designed to help youth make decisions about missions and marriage and repentance, it would be entirely appropriate for parents to first meet with the leaders and ask some very difficult questions about a particular leader's perspective on sexual orientation and see if a relationship of trust and congruence about attitudes regarding sexual orientation, acceptance, and repentance can be agreed upon. If not, it might be necessary to discuss your concerns with a stake president to get the support that you and your child need. Priesthood leaders, like all of us, are still learning and growing in regard to this topic, and sometimes part of the way we sustain them is to help them serve better by being honest and loving when we express our concerns about some of the views they have shared in the past.

It is very difficult to present an example of this complex topic without readers making incorrect assumptions based upon what we leave out; nevertheless, we present the following example as one way a parent and child might interact around these issues at two stages of development.

A Discussion with a Younger Adolescent about Same-Sex Attraction

Kiera, a thirteen-year-old discussing her feelings with her parents because her father sensed she was struggling with something.

Father: Kiera, has something been bothering you?

Kiera: Well, sometimes the other girls in my class make fun of me and call me "butch."

Mother: Ouch, that must hurt (as she hugs her daughter, who seems ready to cry).

Father: I'm so sorry, Kiera. Kids can be so cruel sometimes. Does this happen often?

Kiera: No, only a few times, but it hurts. I'm not even sure exactly what it means but I think they are calling me a lesbian.

Father: Before we talk about what that means, is there something we can do to help you deal with this behavior from the other girls? Do you want us to talk to a teacher?

Kiera: No, that will probably only make it worse. I'm okay. It was just a hard week.

Father: Okay, but keep us posted. We are very willing to help out more directly with the bullying.

Kiera: Thanks. So how does a person know if they are gay or not?

Father: That is a great question and not an easy thing to figure out. It may take many years.

Kiera: Sometimes when I hear my friends get so excited about a boy, I don't get it. He doesn't seem very attractive to me.

Mother: Do you find that you do get excited about how certain girls look and that you feel attracted to them?

Kiera: I'm not sure. Some girls seem prettier and more interesting to me than many boys, who seem immature and stupid.

Father: Well, it sounds like you are not sure what type of people you are attracted to yet and are still figuring things out.

Kiera: Yes, but why don't I feel like so many of the other girls when they see a cute boy?

Mother: Kiera, it is natural for people to have very different feelings about sexual attraction, just like people have different feelings about other things they like, such as music or food or any of our passions. Do you notice how you can really love something and someone else might not like it at all?

Kiera: Like Justin [her brother] never likes the same thing I like!

Father: Exactly. So it is important to not let your friends or others make you worry about who you are attracted to or whether you are weird. Sexual attraction is very unique and different for every one of us in terms of how strong our feelings are and who and what gets us excited. So let's just keep talking about this, and remember people can be cruel about anyone who is even a little bit different than they are.

Kiera: So will I know at some point whether I am gay or not?

Mother: Perhaps it might become clear to you, but there are some people who are attracted to people of both sexes, while others are only attracted to the opposite sex, and some are only attracted to the same sex. So it may not be as clear as you hope or as some others feel. What matters is how we live our lives and whether we keep the commandments so we can have God's Spirit and live together with Him eternally.

A Discussion with a Young Adult about Same-Sex Attraction

Mike, a twenty-one-year-old.

Father: So, Mike, I've noticed you have not been dating much.

Mike: Yeah, I'm pretty busy and I don't like all the games people play.

Father: Are there any other reasons that you might not be interested in dating? I remember us talking about some things when you were younger, but you never really have dated much even after we talked.

Mike: Well, I'm just not very interested or motivated. Maybe I'm gay, Dad! (He chuckles as he says this, but he really is watching his father's reaction to see if it is safe to talk about this sensitive subject.)

Father: Well, you're joking, but is that something you are really wondering about?

Mike: Yes, but I don't feel like talking about it.

Father: I can understand why it would be difficult to talk about, but I imagine you have a lot of pent-up feelings about this if you have been wondering about it for years.

Mike: I'm pretty sure I'm not attracted to women. They have never really interested me. Do you hate me for saying that?

Father: Oh, Mike (giving his son a hug). There is not a single thing you could do that would make me hate you. I feel sad that this is something that is so hard to talk about and that has caused you so much pain.

Mike: Well, I just didn't want to disappoint you and Mom, and I want to do what is right, so I hoped if I just ignored it, it would go away.

Father: So if you are attracted to men, does that mean you are doing something wrong?

Mike: It feels that way. It seems like if I would just pray hard enough and I was righteous enough God would take this from me just like He takes the desire to smoke or do other things from people when they join the Church.

Father: Mike, sometimes God does remove certain temptations from us, but I would guess for every one person who has the desire to smoke removed, there are at least ten who keep struggling with the temptation for the rest of their lives. Especially when we are talking about something as basic as sexual attraction, I would guess that if by now you are not attracted to women, that is probably how things are going to be for you.

Mike: Then what should I do? The other day a friend told me I should just accept who I am and stop pretending to live this religion stuff that is making me miserable.

Father: What do you think?

Mike: Well, I know the Church is true, Dad, and I don't think just tossing it out the window is the solution.

Father: I'm glad to hear that. I think it is possible to be true to your covenants and feel attracted to the same sex. It is not going to be easy, but I think it will be worth it.

A Note to Parents

We began this chapter by discussing how anxious many parents are when they even think about the issues of same-sex attraction, but we have not addressed those feelings and what parents might do to cope with them in a healthy way. Parents often feel intense feelings of sadness, guilt, and sometimes anger or frustration when one of their children experiences same-sex attraction. The feelings often revolve around having to accept that the life they wished for their son or daughter is going to be much more challenging than they had hoped. If they have been willing to be open and loving during the process of accepting that same-sex attraction is going to be a persistent part of their child's life, they have probably cried together many times and tasted directly how difficult this pathway is going to be. Additional sadness can be present depending on the choices their child has decided to make in regard to feelings of same-sex attraction. It may be that parents are giving up dreams of a temple marriage, grandkids, etc. If feelings of sadness persist for more than a few weeks and deepen into feelings of depression, therapeutic help may be necessary.

If there is any area where parents need to talk with others who have experienced similar challenges, this is the area. There are likely friends, ward members, neighbors, and colleagues who are going through similar challenges. Often, finding out that we are not alone and being able to share sorrows and successes with others in similar situations to our own can be a powerful way to work through the difficult feelings and find better ways of coping. Relief Society presidencies and bishoprics are often a good place to start when seeking help, as they will typically know others who are going through similar issues. The Church's materials on the website "Mormon and Gay" (https://mormonandgay.lds.org/) can also be a great place to start the journey to finding a community of support.

It would be wonderful to end this chapter by describing how certain people have successfully navigated the issue of same-sex attraction in their families and everyone lived happily ever after. Same-sex attraction has become a volatile, challenging, and perplexing issue in our society, and we do not expect that this will end anytime soon. Even if families appropriately address and support one another in this area, the responsibility and blessings we have as people of faith to control and express our sexual feelings within heterosexual marriage creates a dissonance between what we believe and how most people act and what many if not the majority of people believe around us. We do feel strongly to leave you with our belief that struggles with sexual orientation can be dealt with in a way that maintains faith and acknowledges each person's uniqueness—that it is possible to live in such a way to be supportive of traditional families and still not discriminate against those who are different. It is possible to be a healthy, happy, and secure individual who is attracted to others of the same sex and be worthy of all the blessings of the gospel. We have also seen parents and families struggling with this issue band together and support one another, and we hope that if this is your situation, you can find others who can walk with you on this difficult path.

While we do not presume that people who are experiencing

same-sex attraction, either personally or vicariously through a close family member or friend, are any more in need of repentance than those who are not, it is certainly likely that the Atonement of Christ will have a specific and unique meaning to them. This is because there is a central aspect of the sufferings of our Savior that was designed to give Christ the power to help us when we are experiencing all manner of pains and afflictions (see Alma 7:11–12). We believe that these aspects of our lives that bring unique challenges and frustrations that are enduring and lifelong merit a specific and special endowment from God as we seek solace and comfort and direction. We hope and pray that you will experience this unique gift and that it will sustain you as you navigate the challenges in your life related to sexuality and sexual attraction.

Chapter Highlights

Having a child who persistently experiences same-sex attraction is rare but common enough that most of us know individuals experiencing these feelings.

While an even smaller subset of individuals experience same-sex attraction and opposite-sex attraction in a more fluid way, this does not mean that individuals choose who will be attractive to them.

There are numerous examples in the media almost on a daily basis that parents could use to initiate discussions about sexual attraction and sexual orientation.

If children have not asked about how someone knows they are gay or wanted to discuss this topic, it is likely that the climate in the home is closed in regard to the topic and that children are turning elsewhere for information and understanding.

Helping children discuss their questions and struggles in

a nonjudgmental way and continuing to love and nurture relationships with them after disclosures of same-sex feelings or behaviors is vital and Christian.

Parents and children both need support systems to help them work through the hard experiences and painful feelings that will accompany same-sex attraction and what this means about living the gospel and making important individual and relational decisions.

Thought Questions

How would you react and feel if someone close to you disclosed that he or she was attracted to people of the same sex? What are the assumptions you might make about that person that might make it harder for him or her to talk to you about this?

If none of your children have ever broached this topic with you, is there some subtle way that you are indicating that it is not a safe topic to discuss in your family?

Putting It into Practice

Parents may want to ask, "Do you have any friends or people you know at school who are homosexual? How do you feel about this? Do you have questions about same-sex attraction? Do people ever ask you about your stance on same-sex relationships or marriage? How do you answer them?"

Parents of children who are experiencing same sex attraction may want to find other parents facing the same issues by asking local leaders for contacts. Parents may be more successful in finding others who have navigated these challenges and sustained faith and hope by contacting local leaders rather than through other forums such as social media, where agendas may be counter to gospel principles.

Chapter 12

Pairing Off and Dating

Too many young people today have boyfriends and girlfriends before they have had boy friends and girl friends.

It's so unfair!" Claudia, a fifteen-year-old sophomore declares as she stares at her parents in the kitchen. "So, just because my birthday is in May I can't go to any school dances?" Her mother tries to tell her that the *For the Strength of Youth* booklet teaches that adolescents shouldn't date until they are sixteen years old, so that is their family rule for dating. But she can see that her daughter's frustration is not soothed with that response. "My friend Emily is soooo immature," retorts Claudia, "but her birthday was in January so she gets to go to the Valentine's dance—why can't I go too?"

"Because that is what the prophet has said," replies Claudia's father.

"But why do we have to wait until we are sixteen—is it some magic age or something?" asks Claudia.

Thinking back to youth lessons she had when she was a teen, Claudia's mom says, "Well, not dating until you are sixteen will help you live the law of chastity."

Showing that quick wit that her parents have come to both love and hate, Claudia snaps, "It's not like anything is going to happen, Mom—it's just a school dance! There are more chaperones there than there are kids."

Trying to draw the conversation to a close, Claudia's father steps in. "You'll understand when you are older, so just stop asking to go to school dances."

Does this conversation sound familiar? We are pretty sure that many parents have had similar exchanges around the initiation of dating in their children's lives. In fact, for years now, as we have met with youth groups throughout the Church, we have asked them, "Is there a right way to date?" Without hesitation, we hear the same response: "Don't date until you're 16!" When we ask them if there is anything more, we are usually met with blank stares. Is that one prescription the sum total of what our teens understand about dating? Unfortunately, we sometimes don't get much better responses when we ask parents the same question.

Another interesting pattern we have seen is that when we ask teens to tell us what they have been taught about dating, they typically tell us about what they learned at the latest etiquette dinner held by their ward youth group. They tell us about table manners, opening doors, and not ignoring your date at the school dance by talking too much with your friends. Now, don't get us wrong, we are big fans of teaching young people about dating etiquette, particularly in this day and age when our kids' cell phones often get more attention than the person sitting in front of them. But waiting until you're sixteen years old to go to high school dances and keeping your elbows off the table aren't exactly the big picture of dating that young people are lacking today. Most importantly, only discussing the *whats* of dating and leaving out the *whys* of dating leaves our children feeling like their parents' opinions and rules about dating are just old-fashioned notions that no one really follows anymore.

In this chapter, we discuss guiding principles for how to teach children about dating and how their approach to dating is indeed connected to living a chaste life before marriage and being ready for the sexual part of a marriage relationship when that time comes. It's important for us to help our children appreciate that healthy dating is much broader than going to dances or bowling—it involves a thoughtful approach to how they pair off or don't pair off during their teenage and early young adult years. Different patterns of pairing off are often linked to how they express themselves physically and sexually in those relationships. As your children come to better understand these principles, they will have greater success in dating and a better chance of making decisions about sex that will bless their dating relationships and later marriages.

Principles of Healthy Dating

As we just mentioned, one of the most common mistakes parents make in teaching their children about dating is they teach them the *whats* or *hows* of dating without sufficiently teaching them the *whys* behind what they are being taught. And as all parents come to know sooner or later, kids want to know the whys! Particularly the whys behind things they are being asked to do that their friends or others may not be doing. One of the most important things you can do as a parent is help your children understand the *purposes* behind any patterns that may be encouraged. At the core, healthy dating is about helping our children delay pairing off and coupling until the young adult years in order to develop the needed maturity to make good relationship decisions. Healthy dating also includes a developmental pattern that helps them manage their sexual feelings and learn to integrate the physical and emotional parts of their sexuality. In sum, the key whys to healthy dating are to promote (1) personal development and maturity, (2) emotionally healthy relationships, (3) sexual restraint before marriage, and (4) sexual readiness in marriage. Let's consider some principles of healthy dating that help to inform the whys of dating.

Principle #1: Pairing Off Is Powerful

Although we have referred to these principles as principles of healthy dating, perhaps the best label for them is "principles for pairing." Encouraging healthy sexuality for our children is about how and when they pair off or couple with others—whether they are on a formal date or not. In fact, more sexual experimentation among teens happens in the "down time" of their lives, such as after school or while hanging out on the weekend, than it does during formal dates. Prophetic counsel to youth in the Church reflects an understanding of the power of pairing, its links to sexuality, and the natural process that emerges as two people begin to spend time together and eventually become a couple. In fact, the power of pairing is recognized as being so powerful that teens are counseled to *not pair off* or form couple relationships, while on the other hand, young adults are encouraged *to pair off* properly to move forward in the courtship process when the time is right.

Premature pairing off is risky, as young people lack the maturity to handle the emotions and intimacies involved with increased attachment and commitment. For young adults, however, pairing off creates the ideal dating environment to get to know potential partners and to evaluate the prospect of their relationship. The most important, and at times the most challenging, aspect of teenage dating is to help our children appreciate how important it is to maintain a *non-coupled status* in dating. One of the most common errors teens make is to become exclusive with one person and to begin to spend a lot of time alone with him or her. While our prophetic leaders warn *young adults* about "hanging out" instead of going on traditional dates, with *teens* there is a different form of "hanging out," and they often do it so they *can* pair off. What this involves is young people telling their parents they are just "hanging out" with a group of friends, and then, when the group is out of sight of parents, the young people pair off into their boyfriend and girlfriend pairs.

Some teens think it is OK to pair off exclusively because they call it "hanging out" instead of dating. Teach your children to not play with definitions. No matter what they call it, it still leads to spending time alone with one person and identifies them as a "couple." If they pair off, the attractions and feelings they will have for that person are the same whether they call it dating, going out, going steady, or hanging out. And in many situations, sexual involvement accompanies these patterns. The sad reality in today's dating culture is that too many young people have boyfriends or girlfriends before they have boy friends or girl friends. This limits our children's social experiences and friendships in ways that hinder their proper preparation for marriage. Plus, premarital sexual experiences can influence their sexual conditioning and attach feelings of guilt, shame, and regret to sexual expression. These are feelings that can negatively impact later sexual intimacy in marriage.

We need to help our children be very wise about the decision to enter into an exclusive relationship with someone. Exclusive dating should always involve an intentional decision, not just waking up one day and "finding" themselves in a committed relationship. This is what researchers call "sliding versus deciding" in relationship formation. When two people become a couple, they change the nature of the relationship between the two of them and the nature of their interactions with others. They stop dating others and no longer gain dating experience of that sort. In order to help our children avoid pairing off too early, it is helpful to encourage them to foster opposite-sex friendships, hanging out in mixed-gender groups, and group dating. All of these patterns will help children develop the capacities needed to form and maintain friendships.

Principle #2: Healthy Dating Starts Earlier Than Many Parents Realize

When we shift our focus to patterns of pairing off and not just formal dating, it becomes clear that encouraging healthy dating and sexual restraint during adolescence is a process that needs to start much earlier than many parents recognize. It is helpful for parents to think of a *pre-dating period* of development, which is intended to help their middle-school-age children develop the capacities they need to form and maintain friendships of various types. If you wait until your child is sixteen to start talking about dating, it will be too late. Another key mistake many parents make during this stage is to not allow their children to have enough proper "boy-girl" social experiences—thus limiting the foundation they have for later dating experiences. Some examples of the types of social interactions that are helpful in the early teens involve having our children attend combined Young Men and Young Women activities in Church youth groups, participating in mixed-gender activities at school and with friends, setting up weekend "hanging out" parties with friends, and attending non-date dances when they turn fourteen. All of these types of experiences will give you a chance as parents to discuss the benefits of opposite-sex friendships and healthy ways that boys and girls can associate together without sexualizing or romanticizing those relationships.

Principle #3: Texting Can Be a Method of Pairing

Many parents are struggling to keep up with the rapidly changing landscape of digital communication that dominates the social culture of teens and young adults today. Often children are being given smartphones and other digital devices at early ages and starting to engage in unmonitored communication with friends, peers, and others. While much of this communication fits into friendship building and social connection, some teens use their phones to engage in private, paired-off, one-on-one communication with members of the opposite sex that mirrors relationship dynamics of dating and exclusive relationships. Some teens are basically "going to bed with each other" as they stay up late texting and talking until they fall asleep. Parents need to recognize the importance of helping their children develop proper patterns of media use and communication with friends and peers during their teenage years. Most teens benefit from clear family values related to phone and technology use, such as "turning in their phones" before going to bed, no phones allowed at the dinner table, and parents having access to their children's phones. As mentioned in Chapter 10, many companies are introducing "accountability software" tools to the market that give parents different ways to monitor and supervise their children's use of media. These approaches are more helpful than filter programs alone, because they give children opportunities to make decisions and be accountable. Plus, they allow parents to set different levels of use permission for children at different age and maturity levels.

Another mistake parents can make is to assume that if their children are at home they cannot be sexually involved with other teens. Recent studies have shown that "sexting" is becoming an increasingly common part of teen culture. The term "sexting" involves sending sexually suggestive text messages or messages with nude or nearly-nude photos. While the majority of attention has been directed toward sexting via cell phone, the term can apply to any digital media, such as email, instant messaging, and social networking sites. The term can be used for producing and sending images of oneself, receiving images directly from the producer, or forwarding received images to other people. One of the first studies on sexting was conducted by the National Campaign to Prevent Teen and Unplanned Pregnancy. The survey found that 20% of teens, ages thirteen to nineteen, including 18% of teen boys and 22% of teen girls, had sent or posted nude or semi-nude pictures or videos of themselves on the Internet or through a cell phone. The majority of teens said they sent sexually suggestive content to boyfriends or girlfriends. However, 21% of teen girls and 39% of teen boys said they sent the content to someone they wanted to date or "hook up" with. Fifteen percent of teens who had sent sexually suggestive content did so to someone they only knew online. These patterns emphasize the importance of parents approaching "dating" with a broader lens and recognizing the variety of ways that teens must learn to manage sexual dynamics in peer and dating relationships.

Principle #4: Encouraging Young Adult Dating

It seems like we regularly hear accounts of how young adults today do not date and all they want to do is hang out with friends and have hookups. Is this true? Our experience and the newest research studies indicate that the answer is both yes and no. It is clear that modern dating in the young adult years involves ample amounts of hanging out and hooking up—and these trends have found their ways to some degree into the LDS young adult culture, too. However, these patterns are overstated at times, and many young adults both inside and outside of the Church are frustrated by the eroded dating culture they experience and often feel helpless to change. Parents and others need to be mindful of these contextual realities as they mentor young people in dating and social experiences.

Our experience is that many young adults feel bombarded by "marriage talk" that condemns hanging-out patterns and emphasizes formal dating aimed at marriage. While the goal of such efforts is a laudable one, we believe that the method is not helping young adults in the ways that they need. In fact, too much emphasis on marriage-oriented dating is paradoxical for many young people in that it makes dating such a big deal that young people retreat rather than step forward. While hanging out is not a good pattern for forming a committed relationship, it does play a needed social function as a way to introduce people to one another and provide informal social support. When properly used, hanging out and broadening one's social circles are important aspects of social development that can lead to healthy dating.

In connection with proper hanging out, parents and others need to encourage young adults to engage in casual paired or one-on-one dating. Rather than prematurely emphasizing marriage, the purposes of this type of dating are to help our children refine their social skills, gain experience with a range of people, and experience interactions with different companions. President Dallin H. Oaks taught, "Simple and more frequent dates allow both men and women to 'shop around' in a way that allows extensive evaluation of the prospects. The old-fashioned date was a wonderful way to get acquainted with a member of the opposite sex. It encouraged conversation. It allowed you to see how you treat others and how you are treated in a one-on-one situation."[1] This type of casual, paired dating is the most endangered form of dating in the modern context. It is the stage that has disappeared the most in the contemporary erosion of courtship. Because of this, our prophetic leaders have begun to counsel young adults in the Church about the importance of paired dating that can one day lead to exclusive dating.

In contrast to the teen years, during young adulthood there should be enough maturity to handle these situations and take advantage of the power of pairing. So the message about pairing to young daters is "slow down," while the message to older daters is "get going!" Following this counsel, we should encourage our children to resist the cultural trend of only two kinds of dating—hanging out or exclusive. Proper dating needs the middle ground of paired dating. For this to happen, we cannot jump to the conclusion that because two people have gone on a couple of dates, there must be something serious going on. Teach your young adult children to allow themselves and others the freedom to pair date without being confronted with questions about commitment and marriage. Emphasizing the importance of becoming well acquainted in dating, President Thomas S. Monson taught, "It is essential that you become well acquainted with the person whom you plan to marry so that you can make certain you are both looking down the same pathway, with the same objectives in mind. It is ever so significant that you do this."[2]

The transition to an exclusive dating status makes two people a couple to each other and to other people. It is important to help our children understand that this stage is an important developmental milestone in a relationship that changes the social and developmental context of the relationship. This transition opens a new social reality that often involves extended families, friends, and others. This transition should happen with open discussion between the partners and a clear understanding by both partners that the relationship has entered an exclusive stage of dating. This transition should not be entered lightly or unintentionally. Nor should the transition to exclusive dating be rushed. Help your children understand that while rushing into exclusivity can be problematic, so can unduly delaying or avoiding exclusivity when the relationship is ready for it. All relationships that appropriately progress toward marriage reach a point where they need to become exclusive to continue progressing. If this step does not happen at the right time, the relationship often stalls and anxiety replaces confidence. If this happens, even a very promising relationship can begin to falter.

The power of pairing requires reciprocity and mutuality to thrive. One of the pitfalls in today's dating culture is what can be called the "half a boyfriend is better than no boyfriend" phenomenon. This occurs when one partner (often the woman) has entered the exclusive dating stage, but the other partner (often the man) is still in the paired dating stage (or he is going back and forth from exclusive dating to paired dating). We should help our children understand that clarity needs to be the rule when it comes to exclusive dating—both when entering the stage and when exiting the stage to return to paired dating with other people. Young adult children need to learn to be mature and open with these matters—it is one of the best indicators that they are ready for the deeper commitments of engagement and marriage.

Principle #5: Emphasize the Whys, Not Just the Whats of Chastity

When it comes to dating, the common question for teens is, "How early can I go?" But as they start dating, one of the most common questions, although often unspoken, is: "How far can I go?" Before we answer this question about physical intimacy, we should step back for a minute and ponder what exactly is being asked when our children and their peers ask how far they can go. The counter question is, "How far until what?" Is the question, "Where is the line before I have sinned and need to confess the behavior to my bishop?" The assumption of this question is that it is OK to be physically involved with someone before marriage as long as it will not get you "in trouble" with the Church or keep you from being able to go on a mission or to the temple. Upon deeper consideration, the question "How far can I go?" reveals a lack of understanding about healthy sexuality. This question is perhaps the prime example of focusing only on the behaviors, and not the motivations, of sexuality.

Unfortunately, part of the reason why our children often only focus on what they can do, or the behaviors of chastity, is because that is too often all we teach them. However, we need our children to come to see that the whys of sexuality are an essential part of good sexual decision making—both before and after marriage. So rather than asking, "How far can I go?" the question becomes, "What do you want sex to mean in your life?" The focus becomes the whys, not simply the whats of physical intimacy. If this is done well, we can help our children gain a better understanding of complete intimacy in couple relationships and the type of intimacy needed in dating and courtship to prepare them for sexual wholeness in marriage. Ultimately, as they come to understand these purposes, they will see why sexual restraint and emotional intimacy are essential aspects of marriage preparation in their dating and engagement relationships.

We have found that an important part of helping young people think more deeply about the motivations and consequences of sexuality involves teaching them about the natural sexual responses of their bodies and the value of "arousal awareness" both before and after marriage. This type of understanding begins with an appreciation of the creation and the divine nature each of us shares with our Heavenly Parents. Each of us is a beloved spirit son or daughter of Heavenly Parents and was created in their image. As offspring of God, our bodies have been created so that we are fully equipped to experience all that our loving Father in Heaven intended for us to experience in this life—which includes sexual arousal and pleasure (see Chapter 5 for more on arousal). Because of this, a needed starting point for developing sexual wholeness is a sound knowledge of how men's and women's bodies function sexually, how to "bridle these passions" prior to marriage, and how to enhance the physical sensations experienced during sexual intimacy in marriage. Teaching our children about how their bodies function sexually can be a beautiful experience that inspires an awe for the majesty of our loving Father in Heaven and a profound appreciation that we have been blessed with physical bodies that can allow us to experience a fullness of joy in this life and in the eternities to come.

A better appreciation of patterns of sexual arousal can help young people make better sexual decisions as they define experiences by outcomes and consequences rather than how they fit on a simple list of behaviors. For example, teens and young adults often debate what actually defines passionate kissing. Is it the length of the kiss that makes it passionate? Is it how open the two people's mouths are when they kiss? Is it French kissing? The behavioral definitions can go on and on. With arousal awareness, an outcome definition rather than a behavioral definition emerges—passionate kissing is any manner of kissing that arouses the sexual response of one or both of the participants. Can you see how this consequence-minded view of chastity answers many of the questions that sometimes arise with our children when only discussing the behavioral aspects of chastity?

Prophets have long taught the standard that sexual relations, or behaviors that purposely arouse and stimulate the sexual response of our bodies, should be reserved for marriage. In the *For Strength of Youth* pamphlet, the First Presidency states, "Physical intimacy between husband and wife is beautiful and sacred. . . . God has commanded that sexual intimacy be reserved for marriage. . . . When you are sexually pure, you prepare yourself to make and keep sacred covenants in the temple. You prepare yourself to build a strong marriage and to bring children into the world as part of an eternal and loving family. . . .

"Never do anything that could lead to sexual transgression. Treat others with respect, not as objects used to satisfy lustful and selfish desires. Before marriage, do not participate in passionate kissing, lie on top of another person, or touch the private, sacred parts of another person's body, with or without clothing. Do not do anything else that arouses sexual feelings. Do not arouse those emotions in your own body. Pay attention to the promptings of the Spirit so that you can be clean and virtuous."[3]

One question that we have heard from young people is, "Since having sexual attraction for my spouse is important after marriage, is it okay to have some arousal responses with that person while dating?" It's important to help our children understand that they will experience attraction to and even physical arousal with others while dating, particularly as they pair off and move into exclusive and engaged dating. They need to know that this is not wrong or inappropriate—in fact, such experiences will help them know they are properly sexually attracted to their future spouse. As they develop body awareness and pay attention to their arousal states, they will be able to make decisions of when to stop or discontinue behaviors that may lead to transgression. A recent family home evening lesson developed by the

Church taught this principle well when it said, "When we often focus on the negative consequences of breaking the law of chastity, it can sometimes be challenging for children to understand that sexual feelings are good. It is important to teach that these feelings are wonderful and can help us develop healthy relationships when they are expressed appropriately. Help your children understand the relationship between the sexual feelings they have or will develop and the sexual behavior that should be reserved for married couples. Teach that sexual feelings are a gift from our Heavenly Father and should be treated with respect."

If we help our children understand these five principles of dating, they will more fully understand not only the how and when of dating but the whys of dating. When youth and adults understand why something should be done, and aren't just fed a list of "cans" and "cannots," they are much more likely to internalize ideas as their own and hold fast to them, even when faced with temptation. This will increase the chances of healthy dating and healthy sexuality both before and during marriage.

Chapter Highlights

Healthy dating is about helping our children delay pairing off and coupling until the young adult years in order for teens to develop the needed maturity to make good relationship decisions. It is also a developmental pattern that helps them manage their sexual feelings and learn to integrate the physical and emotional parts of their sexuality in healthy relationships.

Helping our children have a better appreciation of their patterns of sexual arousal can help them make better sexual decisions as they define experiences by outcomes and consequences rather than how they fit on a simple list of behaviors.

Thought Questions

Can your children explain the reasons behind their dating rules?

How do you feel about boy-girl interactions during the junior high years? Is your child getting enough experiences to be ready for group dating in high school?

Can your child explain the sexual responses of his or her body?

Do you unintentionally teach chastity in a behavioral way? How could you more fully teach the motivations and consequences of chastity?

Putting It into Practice

One of the more effective ways to help children avoid pairing off prematurely in the high school years is to start talking about the importance of being friends long before they are dating. Many TV shows aimed at preteen audiences show teens pairing off and becoming boyfriends and girlfriends. Talk about these media depictions with your children, and discuss what young people are often giving up by getting into exclusive dating relationships in their teens. Emphasize the joys of friendships and the proper timing to couple in their young adult years.

Talk openly with your teens about the natural and normal ways that our bodies initiate arousal when we are attracted to someone. Teach them that these feelings, sensations, and responses are to be expected and do not mean that they have done anything wrong or sinful because they experience them during dating and courtship. Help them appreciate how they can learn to pay attention to their levels of arousal and use this awareness as an "early detection system" that can help them bridle their passions in proper ways prior to marriage (see Chapter 5 for more detail on arousal).

Chapter 13

Engagement and Honeymoon

Congratulations! You're done! Well, not really.

Although this is the last chapter of our book, you may still have lots of questions and concerns. That's great and very normal. There is not a clearly marked path for teaching healthy sexuality, just healthy principles and ideas. We are all going to make mistakes and learn how to improve by trial and error. As parents, we are going to still be learning and growing in the area of sexuality ourselves, so we need to consistently seek to understand these strong passions, thoughts, and feelings and evaluate whether we are moving in a positive direction. That is the perfect perspective to have as you now advise your adult children who are beginning their journey into being a married couple. They will make mistakes. They will learn from those mistakes, improve, and become more loving spouses.

If we have been open with our children about their sexual development, adjustment into marriage will most likely be easier. However, they may still worry too much and set too high of expectations for themselves. Hopefully we have learned and can teach them that anxiety kills sexual desire and perfectionism kills joy. Still, when one of our children reaches the point of getting married, it is a time of joy and rejoicing. It is also the final time parents should plan to talk to their children about their sexual development, since after marriage the boundary around their children's sexuality should be drawn around the new couple, unless the couple decides they have a problem they want to talk to a parent or parents together about to get some help.

So let's talk about a healthy perspective on an engagement and honeymoon and how we as parents can encourage healthy sexual attitudes from the onset of marriage. The Savior taught the principle of going the extra mile, being unselfish, and truly loving those around us. Marriage is the perfect environment to practice this important quality. As our adult children transition into marriage, we can emphasize the need for unselfish service and love. This period marks a time when our children are on the brink of more fully exploring their sexual nature, and a parent's healthy perspective may ease the transition. We have encouraged open and comfortable discussions throughout the book, and if you've been able to do that with your children throughout their lives, this point in time is one of the payoffs. However, if you feel regret that you haven't handled the topic of sex ideally, don't despair! Now is a great time to face it and change it, first by admitting to your adult children that although you didn't understand how to candidly talk about sex, you know it is beautiful and important. Now is a good time to encourage healthy discussions about sexual behavior.

In LDS culture, one main distinction between engagement and honeymoon is that marriage marks the line between appropriate premarital affection and marital sexual activity. Cultural trends outside of the Church have largely eliminated that line. Research indicates that most people engage in sex before marriage. However, research also shows that those who spend more time developing a friendship instead of focusing on physical intimacy have more stable relationships. So how can parents help engaged couples maintain healthy sexual behavior during engagement and after the marriage?

Be positive. No matter the challenges you see in the couple's relationship, focus on the positive. Maintaining a relationship with your child and his or her partner is the best way to influence the couple. If our adult children see us working for their good, they will more readily accept guidance. This is true at every age but seems to be particularly true when working with young adults. Parents can admit that this experience is new and there is a learning curve. So promise to be patient with each other! Engagement is inherently stressful, and that is a good thing. This positive stress allows the couple to see each other's responses in trying situations. Part of this stress is the marked and dramatic departure from premarital abstinence to postmarital sex. This change to sexual expression can be disturbing or challenging for some. However, by and large, most couples successfully make this transition and have enjoyable sexual experiences in marriage. Remind your children that sexual activity is a gift and is intended to bless their marriage.

Be open. We should expect to see increased affection and strong desires for more intimacy from our adult children during engagement. Strong feelings of physical attraction are healthy, and parents should hope those feelings are present. However, parents and adult children also understand the need to keep within safe gospel boundaries. If the couple seems to be struggling with keeping the appropriate boundaries, an invitation to talk about this and provide some guidance about what you did when you were engaged to resist temptation might help.

Consequently, a frank reminder of arousal patterns may be useful with engaged adult children. And not just with your own child—it may be appropriate to sit down with the couple and discuss these principles openly. It may seem awkward, but in the long run, the couple will benefit from your openness. A review on the cascade of natural physical arousal may be a helpful way to let our children know that we understand the sexual desires they're experiencing and that we celebrate those feelings.

The natural sequence of physical arousal begins with the physical attraction partners feel toward each other. This attraction creates a desire to be emotionally connected and affectionate. Touching, hugging, and kissing will encourage sexual arousal that will awaken additional sexual passion and then orgasmic arousal. This is a wonderful natural process that when applied in marriage allows spouses to deepen their connection and affection for each other.

Hopefully, physical attraction is just one of the many reasons a couple decides to marry. Combining physical attraction, deeply held affection, and commitment creates a couple ready to experience the natural phases of arousal. Sexual arousal after marriage is no different than arousal before marriage, with the exception that the couple has fewer restrictions and they may act on their mutual sexual arousal and desire. Sight, touch, smell, taste, and sound all have the capacity to stimulate sexual arousal. But arousal through these means alone is purely physical. Deeper meaning to sexual arousal occurs when our minds are actively engaged and focused in the present moment of intimacy. Touching each other's bodies, talking about their love and the feelings that brought them together, holding each other in a relaxing hug, and focusing on breathing can all be arousing.

The process of sexual arousal is built into our bodies and

occurs instinctively. The reason we warn our children to curtail arousal before marriage is because arousal is instinctive. It occurs naturally in a course of progression that is typically difficult to slow down. That fact can be comforting news for a soon-to-be-married couple—this is a natural process. It may be good to also review how men's and women's arousal patterns are different. Parents could bolster their children's base of information by reviewing Chapters 7–11 of the book *Sexual Wholeness in Marriage: An LDS Perspective on Integrating Sexuality and Spirituality in Our Marriages.*[1]

To help a young couple maintain their standards during engagement, some additional boundaries may be needed. Parents can discuss with their children ways to be supportive. Is it helpful to have a set time to separate at night? Would the couple feel good about having a chaperone in the house instead of being home alone together (a younger brother or sister would do)? The goal is to help the couple realize that the family is there to help in any appropriate way. Openness to the realities of sexual attraction during engagement will go a long way toward preventing premarital sexual overreaching.

Encourage a healthy honeymoon. The honeymoon is a time set apart for couples to get to know each other physically. Expensive vacation sites or glamorous hotels are not the purpose of a honeymoon. A honeymoon is actually a very important time where the cares of work, family, and other obligations can be temporarily suspended and a physical relationship explored in greater depth.

Hopefully the young couple can understand as they approach their honeymoon that sex is not about individual gratification but about giving to their spouse. A sexual relationship is about mutual enjoyment, enrichment, and bonding of the couple. Newlyweds who approach sex with their spouse in mind will experience more rewarding sex—guaranteed! The bride or groom who approaches the honeymoon as simply the time to satisfy their own desires not only misses an opportunity for greater emotional closeness and deeper physical meaning but creates the possibility of real emotional hurt.

Parents can explain that sex is a wonderful physical union that impacts our body, spirit, and emotions. Sex allows two people, committed to help each other despite the naturally resulting struggles and disappointments of mortality, to come together to build and nurture each other. While sexual expression in marriage has the incredible capacity to create mortal bodies for spirits coming to earth, on a more regular basis, it has the potential to generate an atmosphere of creative fun, establish a pattern of nurture and acceptance, create calm for troubled hearts, and heal the hurts of daily living. It is helpful to let the new couple know that just like learning anything new, they should be patient with themselves and encourage a sense of lightheartedness over mishaps as they embark on this sexual journey together.

Answers to Common Questions

As parents we may be blessed to answer questions of concern for our adult children. Every couple has questions. They may not feel comfortable blurting them out, but they definitely have questions about sex. Parents can set a number of scheduled times with their child and the fiancé(e) to discuss sexual wholeness in marriage. Don't require them to prompt the discussion. Parents can lead out and have a list of important topics for discussion. Here are a few common topics parents could cover:

Do we need to have intercourse on the wedding night?

No. Sex is intended to be a joyful experience rather than

an overwhelming pressure. The expectation of sexual activity after marriage can be troubling for some. What is the magic switch that makes sex forbidden the day before the wedding and acceptable the next day? Although they now have God's blessing to engage in sexual activity, having sex on the wedding night is not required. The wedding night and beyond is a time to explore this new area of sexual expression. It is intended to be fun, uniting, and fulfilling. They have hopefully developed the foundation of an emotional and spiritual attachment to each other that will continue to develop as they create a physical attachment. Now they can give everything they have to each other—emotionally, spiritually, and physically.

The real goal of sex is intimacy, not sexual intercourse or orgasm. Because intimacy is the real goal, couples usually need to learn to sexually pace their experience so that intimacy increases. Good communication skills will help couples find a pace that is good for them. Slowing the pace is especially critical for newlyweds. The sexual pace should move at the slowest rate necessary for each partner to feel comfortable. In fact, moving slower rather than faster will benefit both partners, as it gives time to experience new feelings and explore each other's ideas about sexuality. If intercourse is the only goal, the couple will miss out on the depth of this initial sexual experience.

Having a plan to move at the pace of the least comfortable partner is far more appropriate than starting your honeymoon with a goal of sexual intercourse. The former creates trust, unity, and closeness. The latter is simply selfish and will do nothing to build the relationship. Remember that the same sexual act that lifts, strengthens, and enlightens a relationship can also oppress, weaken, and obscure the joy of the relationship.

It all depends on whether you are thinking of your spouse or yourself as you accelerate your sexual activity.

Some people have the idea that women move too slowly sexually and that this is a problem. Nothing could be further from the truth. It is no mistake that Heavenly Father creates men and women with different sexual arousal patterns. Men are typically quickly aroused and desire sex more frequently. Women's arousal differs in that arousal is usually slower, may last longer, and is more sensitive to the environment of the relationship. If the couple is working to satisfy both arousal patterns, their sexual experience will attend to each person's arousal and be deeper and more fulfilling for both the man and the woman. Satisfying sex results from partners who are willing to work on the relationship and regularly make time for attentive sex. We can remind our children of the message they have hopefully heard many times before: sexual wholeness is the goal. Developing emotional and spiritual intimacy is just as important as developing physical intimacy.

Is sex just to create babies?

No, sex is not JUST to create children. Sex plays a number of very important roles in a marriage. Certainly a great result of sex is a child, but the vast majority of sexual experiences in a marriage are not to procreate—they are to create a strong union between spouses. Sex on the honeymoon can establish an atmosphere of creativity, fun, and deepening the sexual relationship beyond the physical, drawing in the mental and the spiritual. This is what we refer to as sexual wholeness. Sexual wholeness is fun. Sexual wholeness is happy. Sexual wholeness is not simply pleasurable but also nourishing, powerful, and healing. It is not just arousing. It is emotionally satisfying. Sexual wholeness is an opportunity to share ideas and hopes with each other. It is a dimension of each person that has not been fully explored until this time. Finding ways to be playful, learn likes and dislikes, and explore their own eroticism takes time and practice.

Earlier, we mentioned that sex is as much mental as it is physical. Because of that, sexual arousal affects not only the physiological makeup of the genitals; it also affects the physiology of the brain. It is helpful to understand this. During arousal and orgasm, the chemistry of our brain changes because oxytocin levels in our brains increase during sex. High levels of oxytocin do at least two things to the brain: first, they create brain plasticity (an ability to change and remap the pathways of the brain); and second, they generate feelings of attachment.

For example, research indicates the interaction between a nursing mother and her child raises oxytocin levels in the mother's brain. The mother's increased levels of oxytocin increase after birth and during nursing to increase the process of attachment. It's a beautiful part of Heavenly Father's plan to create strong family attachments. Increases in oxytocin play an important part in sex as well. Sexual arousal releases oxytocin to our brains. Like the mother/child relationship, the sexual partners form attachments to each other. Through that process (higher levels of arousal), we create and strengthen emotional attachments to our partner. This too is part of a perfect plan of a loving Heavenly Father to fortify couples, by strong attachment, against the unavoidable trials of marriage and life. When a young couple committed by marriage engage in sex, they are strengthening the attachment they feel toward each other. Within marriage this increase in attachment is healthy and protective.

Couples who desire to give everything to each other will create an environment of healthy sex, which will lead to a stronger relationship, which naturally leads to happier family life. This increased attachment is a beautiful demonstration of Heavenly Father's love and protection created in our intimate relationships when we respect sacred guidelines that honor our sexuality. Because of this, healthy intimacy buffers couples against the normal bumps and trials that occur within marriage.

What are the mechanics of sex?

Some couples are concerned that because they have not been sexually active, they will not know enough to have sex. Despite the built-in instinctive physical responses, it is helpful to know the mechanics of sex, gender differences, and the process of developing a satisfying relationship. If you have not yet discussed maturation with your child, it would be a good time to refer back to Chapter 5 and help the couple understand the physical differences between men and women and how these will impact their sexual experience. You might even discuss different sexual positions and how some might be more helpful for female orgasm than others, while always encouraging the couple to communicate and be patient with one another as they discover the ways to pleasure each other sexually. As parents, we can comfort our children by reminding them that both men and women are aroused visually. Seeing your partner dressed or undressed is a stimulant and will bring on a cascade of natural arousal, mentioned above. In addition to visual arousal, touch is arousing. Couples who before marriage only kissed, hugged, and held hands are now able to explore each other's bodies more freely. Touching will naturally lead to higher levels of arousal, causing men to have erections and women to lubricate. This process of arousal can be taken at a pace that is deliberately slow so that each couple can process the experience and feel comfortable, not rushed into higher levels of arousal.

Sometimes inexperienced young men may have a difficult time pacing their arousal and may prematurely ejaculate. Or the couple may rush their arousal and attempt penetration before the woman is fully ready, causing unnecessary pain. Taking a slow, intentional approach creates a better experience for both. If these mishaps occur, couples who understand that this is part of the learning process can laugh with each other and prepare for the next opportunity to practice, armed with a little better understanding of how their bodies work together. This physical exploration should be enjoyable and has no predetermined timetable. Think of each other and discover how your bodies respond to each other. Parents can reassure their young adult children that sex is a fun adventure. However, even though sex is simple, it is also complicated, and it takes years to understand the nuances of how sex works in any relationship. That is one of the beautiful parts of sex! We need to practice all these great ideas! As we learn to be better tuned in to our spouse, our sexual experiences become more meaningful and bonding.

How often should we have sex?

Intercourse should never be demanded, and realistic expectations should be informed by the couple's relationship—not by popular sex ideas. Too often couples are interested in the "averages" of sex. How often should we have sex? How long is an orgasm? How do I achieve the best orgasm? Do we both have to orgasm every time we have sex? Should we orgasm at the same time? These questions entirely miss the point of intimate sex. The more appropriate questions are: How can I share authentic feelings with my spouse? How can I be aware of her/his needs and feelings? How can I make this a better experience for my spouse? These questions can only be answered by the couple, and discussions like this will create an environment that increases sexual intimacy.

Not all parents can talk this openly about sexual intercourse with their adult children, but this is the goal. So, be brave, work through your own sexual struggles first, and try to gain as much openness as possible. You are helping them create a healthy foundation. Our children are bound to have problems in marriage, which is part of the process of becoming one. Sexual problems often require careful attention to the entire relationship. Letting our children see that we value sexual wholeness and understand the complexities and beauty of sex will encourage them to look for happy, healthy solutions to problems in their marriage and sexual development.

Chapter Highlights

Be open and positive about your adult child's coming marriage. Sit down and visit about arousal patterns and how bodies are designed to respond to sexual stimulation. Review the differences in men's and women's arousal.

Encourage a simple honeymoon that allows time to get to know each other physically. This is a time for healthy exploration. Part of the fun is in the learning. Spouses help teach each other what is enjoyable and unifying.

Remember that being other-focused will create the best sexual experiences. Intimacy includes far more than just sex. Emotional and spiritual connectedness are important elements of sexual wholeness.

Thought Questions

How do you feel about discussing sexuality with your adult child and his or her fiancé(e)? Did your parents have a similar discussion with you? How does that impact your willingness to try?

How does your understanding of sexual wholeness and the mistakes you have made in your own marriage impact your willingness or ability to discuss these issues with your child?

Research finds that young adult children benefit from a close emotional relationship with their parents. How will you maintain this relationship while allowing your child to cleave to his or her spouse?

Putting It into Practice

Schedule several "sex talks" with your child and his or her soon-to-be spouse. Make them fun and allow these young adults to ask questions and let you know what they might like to talk about. Have a follow-up discussion after they have been able to think about these issues more fully—they may have additional questions. Have the engaged couple write down their questions if they are less comfortable discussing these topics.

Review Chapter 5 with the couple. Are they aware of the purposes of each part of the male and female body? This does not need to be a quiz, but generally review the incredible nature of men's and women's bodies and how a baby is created and why sex is enjoyable.

Ask the couple to discuss the importance of intimacy outside of sex. How will emotional and spiritual intimacy impact their physical intimacy? How does tending to the quality of their relationship impact their sexual relationship?

Discuss the differences in how men and women are sexually aroused. If needed, refer to Chapter 11 in *Sexual Wholeness in Marriage: An LDS Perspective on Integrating Sexuality and Spirituality in Our Marriages*. Explain that women often need more time to become aroused and that this difference between men and women can actually enhance the sexual experience.

Notes

Introduction

1. Bradley D. Foster, "It's Never Too Early and It's Never Too Late," *Ensign*, Nov. 2015.

Chapter 1: Sexual Metaphors

1. Cheryl A. Esplin, "Teaching Our Children to Understand," *Ensign*, May 2012.
2. C. Scott Grow, "The Miracle of the Atonement," *Ensign*, May 2011.

Chapter 2: Moving beyond Abstinence toward Sexual Wholeness

1. Jeffrey R. Holland, "Of Souls, Symbols, and Sacraments," BYU Devotional, 12 Jan. 1988.
2. "The Family: A Proclamation to the World," *Ensign*, Nov. 2010.
3. Dallin H. Oaks, "Apostasy and Restoration," *Ensign*, May 1995.
4. Bruce C. and Marie K. Hafen, *The Belonging Heart: The Atonement and Relationships with God and Family* (Salt Lake City: Deseret Book, 1994), 9–11.

Chapter 3: Parents Are Integral

1. Larry R. Lawrence, "Courageous Parenting," *Ensign*, Nov. 2010.
2. Susan W. Tanner, "Did I Tell You . . . ?" *Ensign*, May 2003.
3. Lawrence, "Courageous Parenting."
4. Sharon G. Larsen, "Fear Not: For They That Be with Us Are More," *Ensign*, Nov. 2001.

Chapter 4: Parenting Is Different for Different Children

1. Elaine S. Dalton, "We Are Daughters of Our Heavenly Father," *Ensign*, May 2013.
2. Dieter F. Uchtdorf, "The Love of God," *Ensign*, Nov. 2009.

Chapter 5: Basics of Sexual Anatomy and Puberty

1. Jörg Klebingat, "Approaching the Throne of God with Confidence," *Ensign*, Nov. 2014.

Chapter 6: Discussing and Celebrating Puberty

1. Horacio A. Tenorio, "Let Us Build Fortresses," *Ensign*, Nov. 1994.
2. David A. Bednar, "More Diligent and Concerned at Home," *Ensign*, Nov. 2009.

Chapter 7: Body Image

1. Jeffrey R. Holland, "To Young Women," *Ensign*, Nov. 2005.
2. Holland, "To Young Women."
3. Susan W. Tanner, "The Sanctity of the Body," *Ensign*, Nov. 2005.
4. Russell M. Nelson, "Decisions for Eternity," *Ensign*, Nov. 2013.
5. Boyd K. Packer, "Ye Are the Temple of God," *Ensign*, Nov. 2000.

Chapter 8: Modesty and Sexuality

1. Carol F. McConkie, "Courage to Choose Modesty," *Ensign*, Nov. 2014.
2. Linda K. Burton, "We'll Ascend Together," *Ensign*, May 2015.
3. McConkie, "Courage to Choose Modesty."

Chapter 9: Self-Touching and Masturbation

1. Jeffrey R. Holland, "Tomorrow the Lord Will Do Wonders among You," *Ensign*, May 2016.
2. Sheri L. Dew, "Our Only Chance," *Ensign*, May 1999.

Chapter 10: Pornography

1. Jeffrey R. Holland, "Place No More for the Enemy of My Soul," *Ensign*, May 2010.
2. Dallin H. Oaks, "Recovering from the Trap of Pornography," *Ensign*, Oct. 2015.

Chapter 11: Same-Sex Attraction

1. D. Todd Christofferson, "Love One Another: A Discussion on Same-Sex Attraction," from the website mormonandgay.lds.org.
2. Dallin H. Oaks, "Love and Law," *Ensign*, Nov. 2009.
3. Jeffrey R. Holland, "Behold Thy Mother," *Ensign*, Nov. 2015.

Chapter 12: Pairing Off and Dating

1. Dallin H. Oaks, "Dating versus Hanging Out," *Ensign*, June 2006.
2. Thomas S. Monson, "Whom Shall I Marry?" *New Era*, Oct. 2004.
3. *For the Strength of Youth* (booklet, 2011), "Sexual Purity."

Chapter 13: Engagement and Honeymoon

1. Dean M. Busby, Jason S. Carroll, and Chelom Leavitt, *Sexual Wholeness in Marriage: An LDS Perspective on Integrating Sexuality and Spirituality in Our Marriages* (Brigham City, UT: Brigham Distributing, 2014).

Bibliography

Bailey, J. Michael, Paul L. Vasey, Lisa M. Diamond, S. Marc Breedlove, Eric Vilain, and Marc Epprecht. "Sexual Orientation, Controversy, and Science." *Psychological Science in the Public Interest* 17, no. 2 (2016): 45–101.

Butler, Mark, in Lisa Ann Jackson Thomson. "Arm Your Kids for the Battle," *BYU Magazine*, Spring 2015.

Carroll, Jason S., Laura M. Padilla-Walker, Larry J. Nelson, Chad D. Olson, Carolyn Mcnamara Barry, and Stephanie D. Madsen. "Generation XXX." *Journal of Adolescent Research* 23, no. 1 (2008): 6–30.

Cash, Thomas F., and Linda Smolak. *Body Image: A Handbook of Science, Practice, and Prevention.* New York, NY: Guilford Press, 2012.

Collins, W. Andrew, and Laurence Steinberg. "Adolescent Development in Interpersonal Context." *Handbook of Child Psychology*, 2007.

Fiese, Barbara H. *Family Routines and Rituals.* New Haven: Yale University Press, 2006.

Gottman, John and Julie. "An Open Letter on Porn." The Gottman Institute. April 5, 2016. Accessed May 2017. https://www.gottman.com/blog/an-open-letter-on-porn/.

Hafen, Bruce C., and Marie K. Hafen. *The Belonging Heart: The Atonement and Relationships with God and Family.* Salt Lake City, UT: Deseret Book Co., 1994.

Hensel, Devon J., and J. Dennis Fortenberry. "Life-span Sexuality through a Sexual Health Perspective." *APA Handbook of Sexuality and Psychology, Vol. 1: Person-Based Approaches.*: 385-413.

Kagan, Jerome. "Temperamental Contributions to Inhibited and Uninhibited

Profiles." In Zelazo, Philip David. *The Oxford Handbook of Developmental Psychology. Self and Other*. New York, NY: Oxford University Press, 2013.

Kochanska, Grazyna, Nazan Aksan, and Mary E. Joy. "Children's Fearfulness as a Moderator of Parenting in Early Socialization: Two Longitudinal Studies." *Developmental Psychology* 43, no. 1 (2007): 222–37.

Lamb, Sharon, and Aleksandra Plocha. "Sexuality in Childhood." *APA Handbook of Sexuality and Psychology, Vol. 1: Person-Based Approaches.*: 415–432.

Markey, Charlotte N. *Smart People Don't Diet: How Psychology, Common Sense, and the Latest Science Can Help You Lose Weight Permanently.* New York: De Capo Lifelong Books, 2014.

Nathanson, Amy I. "The Unintended Effects of Parental Mediation of Television on Adolescents." *Media Psychology* 4, no. 3 (2002): 207–30.

O'Sullivan, Lucia F. and Ashley E. Thompson. "Sexuality in adolescence." *APA Handbook of Sexuality and Psychology, Vol. 1: Person-Based Approaches.*: 433–486.

Oettingen, Gabriele. *Rethinking Positive Thinking: Inside the New Science of Motivation.* New York: Current, 2015.

Robinson, Clyde C., Barbara Mandleco, Susanne Olsen Roper, and Craig H. Hart, "The Parenting Styles and Dimensions Questionnaire (PSQD)." *Handbook of Family Measurement Techniques:* Vol. 3. Instruments and index (2001): 319–21.

Smith, Melissa H. "The Complex Client: Eating Disorders in Midlife." Presented at the Utah Chapter of International Association of Eating Disorder Professionals (IAEDP), University of Utah (November 2017).

Wiederman, Michael W. and Sabina Sarin. "Body Image and Sexuality." *Principles and Practice of Sex Therapy*, 5th ed. (2014): 359–74.

About the Authors

Laura M. Padilla-Walker is a professor in the School of Family Life and an Associate Dean of the College of Family, Home, and Social Sciences at Brigham Young University. Her research focuses on parenting, adolescent sexuality, media, and moral development.

Dean M. Busby is the director of the School of Family Life at Brigham Young University. He has recently been teaching the healthy sexuality in marriage course at BYU. His research has garnered university and national awards and been funded by federal and state grants and has been presented to scholarly and lay audiences around the world.

Chelom E. Leavitt is an assistant professor in the School of Family Life at Brigham Young University and studies sexuality and mindfulness. She received her PhD in human development and family studies from Penn State.

Jason S. Carroll is a professor in the School of Family Life at Brigham Young University and a Fellow of the Wheatley Institution. He is an internationally-recognized researcher and educator in the areas of marriage fragmentation, sexual intimacy, and marriage readiness.

A comprehensive description of sexual wholeness and counsel for building a healthy sexual relationship in marriage can be found in the authors' book *Sexual Wholeness in Marriage: An LDS Perspective on Integrating Sexuality and Spirituality in Our Marriages.*